Cultural Competence

Taking a strategic imperative perspective, this book introduces business leaders to a key differentiator that contributes to competitive advantage and financial sustainability: cultural competence. In a fast-changing and globalized world where organizations are being forced to rethink their strategies, understanding present and future environmental, social, and economic challenges is fundamental to creating a resilient and value-creating business. Combining experience and reflection, this book addresses concepts of organizational cultural competence as an internal differentiator and source of competitive advantage. Most organizations approach differentiation as an external feature of product and/or service delivery. Whereas these are open to imitation, cultural competence, as the internal DNA of an organization, is much more difficult, if not impossible, to imitate. The authors bring to bear their years of experience in corporate roles and as entrepreneurs and academics, sharing views and experiences based on research but also on primary examples, meta-insights, and real-world case studies. Senior leaders and consultants across industries, as well as students of strategy and leadership development, will value this serious and comprehensive guide that explains the importance of cultural competence as a strategic advantage in a global market.

Steyn Heckroodt, PhD, is a practitioner, professor, and thought leader in leadership and strategy, Heckroodt provides a wealth of experience and expertise when engaging with global business leaders in the boardroom, classroom, on the field, and in the cloud. Leveraging on his experience in over 50 countries, consulting for a myriad of organizations, and engaging with tumultuous culturally different workforces, Heckroodt focuses on diversity as the key to intrinsic strategic competitiveness for organizations, hence Cultural Competence.

Waddah S. Ghanem Al Hashmi, BEng (Hons), MBA, MSc, DBA, MIoD, FBDIGCC, is an environmental engineer with a double master's in both sciences and business administration, Waddah has published widely as an Industrial Academic. He is respected as a leading authority on health, safety, environmental and sustainability governance, and leadership, and is also the chairman of the Platform for Connected Leadership. His interest in cultural competence is deeply rooted in his views on the importance of creating a dialogue amongst civilizations, rejoicing in what connects humankind, rather than what differentiates it.

Cultural Competence

The Intrinsic Strategic Advantage

**Steyn Heckroodt and
Waddah S. Ghanem Al Hashmi**

Routledge
Taylor & Francis Group

NEW YORK AND LONDON

Cover image: © maonakub / Adobe Stock Images

First published 2024
by Routledge
605 Third Avenue, New York, NY 10158

and by Routledge
4 Park Square, Milton Park, Abingdon, Oxon, OX14 4RN

Routledge is an imprint of the Taylor & Francis Group, an informa business

ISBN: 978-1-032-30080-1 (hbk)
ISBN: 978-1-032-30077-1 (pbk)
ISBN: 978-1-003-30338-1 (ebk)

DOI: 10.4324/9781003303381

Typeset in Optima
by MPS Limited, Dehradun

Dedicated to our friend, Marjo Louw

Covid might have stolen you from us, but your love, inspiration and legacy will remain forever.

Contents

List of Figures   *ix*

List of Tables   *xi*

Foreword   *xii*

About the Authors   *xiv*

Purpose and Value of this Book   *xvi*

Introduction   1

1 Cultural Competence: A Drop of Ink in a Glass of Water   10

2 The Imperativeness of Culture in Cultural Competence   20

3 Castling: Cultural Competence as a Strategic Differentiator   32

4 The Satya Nadella Case for Cultural Competence   48

5 The Cultural Competence Index (CCI) Measurement Matrix   57

6 Case Study Example Explanations of the CCI Construct Elements   71

7 Institutionalizing Cultural Competence   80

8 Future Challenges and Opportunities for Cultural
Competence 89

Epilogue 95

Bibliography 99
Index 102

Figures

1.1 Ackoff's Data, Information, Knowledge, and Wisdom Model. Illustration created by Marina van Zyl   1

2.1 The Cultural Competence Realm: Amended (Porter, 2008). Illustration created by Marina van Zyl   23

2.2 Different Profit-Centric Strategy Approaches: Amended (Oberholzer-Gee, 2021). Illustration created by Marina van Zyl   25

2.3 Strategic Approach beyond Standard Approaches. Illustration created by Marina van Zyl   26

3.1 Strategy Continuum Framework: Amended (Lafley & Martin, 2013). Illustration created by Marina van Zyl   33

3.2 Strategy as a Positioning Act. Illustration created by Marina van Zyl   39

3.3 Strategic Positioning Dimensions (Lafley & Martin, 2013). Illustration created by Marina van Zyl   40

3.4 The Organization as a System. Illustration created by Marina van Zyl   43

4.1 Evolution of Microsoft's Stock Price. Illustration created by Marina van Zyl   50

4.2 Cultural Competence Index Measurement Matrix. Illustration created by Marina van Zyl   55

5.1 Complete Combined CCI Measurement Matrix. Illustration created by Marina van Zyl   60

5.2 Constructs Applicable to External Stakeholder Loyalty. Illustration created by Marina van Zyl   62

5.3 Constructs Applicable to Internal Stakeholder Loyalty. Illustration created by Marina van Zyl   63

5.4   Classification Matrix – Supplier/Landlord. Illustration
      created by Marina van Zyl   66
5.5   CCI Simplified. Illustration created by Marina
      van Zyl   69
7.1   Business Model: Amended (Johnson, Christensen, &
      Kagermann, 2008). Illustration created by Marina
      van Zyl   81
7.2   Kotter's Eight Step Process (Kotter, 2012). Illustration
      created by Marina van Zyl   83
7.3   Kanter's Change Wheel (Kanter, 2011). Illustration
      created by Marina van Zyl   86
7.4   Organizational Activity Systems: Amended (Dostal,
      Cloete, & Jaros, 2005). Illustration created by Marina
      van Zyl   88

Tables

5.1 Results of CM on Supplier Performance Cultural
    Competence Dimension   67
6.1 Results of CM on Staff Performance Cultural
    Competence Dimension   77

Foreword

My interest in cultural competence was sparked during my time as Head of Legal Services for a large local company in the United Arab Emirates. I was an expatriate, one of two females, in a leadership position and worked with 300 employees from 40 different nationalities. From a diversity standpoint, the organization was complying on all levels. From an inclusion perspective, it needed some work though. The missing link – cultural competence.

Fast forward a year and a half and I had developed, with the leadership of the organization, a thorough diversity and inclusion program that attempted to thread into each aspect of the organization an understanding of what made us unique from a cultural perspective, a process for testing that understanding and a dedicated committee to work with the business to use that unique cultural perspective to drive the business, enhance employee engagement, and make the organization a recruiter of first choice.

It was during this period that I met the authors of this book and was fascinated with their proposal to create a system that any organization can use to develop, enhance, and maintain their cultural programs – the Cultural Competence Index (CCI). If only such a manual had existed while I was developing my organization's program!

The importance of cultural competence cannot be understated. It can make or break a company in the same way as financial success or failure. However, it is rare that organizations have the insight to comprehend this before reaching a critical point where staff morale is at rock bottom, the organization's reputation is on the line and large salaries and financial incentives are no longer sufficient to maintain talent.

Organizations also generally fail to understand that cultural competence has no correlation to national culture – if it did, a female expat in a Gulf company could not effect meaningful change. The authors demonstrate in this book the importance of cultural competence, the benefits to an organization to achieving that competence, and provide a framework within which to develop a business culture that is unique and cannot be copied – resulting in enhanced competitiveness and increased profits.

So, why this book – the authors give a clear structure for how to assess cultural competence in a business while allowing for individualized application. It is not a one size fits all approach. It is a roadmap to allow organizations to assess what is important for their business to successfully become culturally competent in whichever area, country, or business they may be. It provides a unique opportunity for businesses to develop their own individual cultural program that cannot be copied or replicated by competitors, and which will drive performance and results.

The importance of such a book in a post-Covid world cannot be understated. Covid, through remote working and digitization, significantly reduced the human element of organizations across the globe and made strategies, to maintain or improve morale more complicated. The Team Building days that most organizations used as a band-aid for their lack of a cultural competence could no longer take place. The culture of all organizations was negatively impacted, and organizations need to take meaningful actions to restore balance.

A point that the authors make several times in this book, and that is absolutely key, is that building a culturally competent organization is not a one-time fix. As with the financial and operative aspects of a business, it needs to be nurtured, maintained, and developed along with the organization. Cultural performance needs to become part of the governance of an organization and be refreshed and reassessed regularly – become as habitual as reviewing profit and loss statements or the business plan.

It is also a matter that needs to be addressed and assessed internally – by the people in the organization that know it best. Expensive consultants cannot test the pulse of an organization, establish the morale of its employees, or get the all-important buy-in from management. It requires a team that employees trust will have their best interests at heart, who care about the success of the business and who can stand behind whatever actions or changes are affected.

It is daunting and difficult to effect meaningful cultural change in an organization, but the benefits are innumerable. This book distills the most difficult parts of creating that change into a metric that any organization can use to drive change.

It is a must-read for all organizations regardless of their type of business, country of establishment, or size.

Ms Nadia Bardawil
Chief Legal Council to Tabreed
Abu Dhabi, United Arab Emirates

About the Authors

Professor Steyn Heckroodt
As Practitioner and Thought Leader in Leadership and Strategy; Heckroodt provides a wealth of experience and expertise when engaging with global business leaders in the room, on the field, and in the cloud. As a HBS Publishing Moderator, HBR Author, Dean, and Co-Founder of Platform for Connected Leadership, he influences leaders globally in shaping the future of the organizations they lead.

The impact he leaves is best known for the focus he places on strategy and how to constantly improve the holistic competitive sustainability of organizations. As complexity enfolds the world of work leaders find themselves in today, Heckroodt shifted his focus more toward diversity, as opposed to expertise, in addressing such complexity. Leveraging on his travels to more than 50 countries in his lifetime, consulting for a myriad of organizations, and engaging with tumultuous culturally different workforces, Heckroodt discovered the strategic differentiator of cultural competence.

Reflecting on the impact of evolving Industrial Revolutions, a 'Work-from-Anywhere' generation, a Disrupting Exabyte Economy, and so much more, Heckroodt turns to cultural competence as the embodying of diversity within organizations, co-contributing an internal competitive strategic differentiator, spreading like a drop of ink through a glass of water.

Dr. Waddah S. Ghanem Al Hashmi FIEMA, FIIRSM, FEI, FBDIGCC, MIoD
An environmental engineer by training with a double master's in both sciences and business administration who has spent more than 25 years starting in consulting and then soon after the energy industry in several technical and senior executive roles. He is a certified director and sits on several international

boards. His research area over the past decade has been in Governance and Leadership and the making of high-reliability organizations. He is the Chairman of the Federal Occupational Safety and Health Standards Committee, and a published author of more than eight international books, two focused on governance and leadership published by Routledge in 2017 and 2021 respectively. He also has published many articles including two articles by the Harvard Business Review Arabia. His doctoral research was focused on EHS Governance and Leadership in High-Risk Organizations and explored perspectives from the GCC region.

Dr. Waddah is also a visiting faculty at the University of Technolgi Petronas (Malaysia) and Hult Business School. He is an external examiner at the University of Petroleum and Energy Sciences (India) and sits on the Industrial Advisory Boards at Herriot Watt University and the University of Abu Dhabi. Waddah is considered one of the authorities on health, safety, environmental, and sustainability governance and leadership. He is also the Chairman of the Platform for Connected Leadership.

His interest in cultural competence and cultural understanding is deeply rooted in his strong views on the importance of creating a dialogue amongst civilizations, rejoicing in what connects humankind rather than what humankind may think always differentiates.

Purpose and Value of this Book

Coincidently, on the day that the authors put pen to paper to conceptualize the purpose and importance of this book, social media was exploding with posts related to the passing of one of the greatest leaders the world ever experienced, the late Archbishop Desmond Tutu.

> Desmond Mpilo Tutu was a South African Anglican bishop and theologian, known for his work as an anti-apartheid and human rights activist. He received both the Nobel Peace Prize for his role as a unifying leader-figure in the non-violent campaign to resolve the problem of apartheid in South Africa and the Gandhi Peace Prize in recognition of his invaluable contribution toward social and political transformation and forging equality in South Africa through the Gandhian values of dialogue and tolerance.

On pondering over the words' purpose and importance, it dawned on the authors that what makes a great leader, like the Tutus of the World, is the ability to bring about change, for the better, through a deep-centered value of respect, across all cultures. The quote of the great Muhammed Ali, also came to mind, when he said: *Service to others is the rent you pay for your room here on earth.* (Muhammad Ali, Feb 27, 1978, Time Magazine).

What greatness within one must have to be the number one boxing heavyweight champion of the world, and display such humility, kindness, and be such an inspiration to bring about change in people.

> Muhammad Ali was an American professional boxer and activist. Nicknamed 'The Greatest,' he is regarded as one of the most significant sports figures of the 20th century and is frequently ranked as the greatest heavyweight boxer of all time. After he grew

close to Malcolm X, the African American Muslim Minister and human rights activist, he renounced the name 'Clay' citing it as a slave name. Concerned that he would stray from the Nation of Islam, Elijah Muhammad, an American religious leader, offered him a new name to secure his allegiance: 'Muhammad Ali.'

It is in this metaphor that the authors argue and defend the importance and purpose of this book. In line with the philosophies of many great leaders, this book is aimed at making changes, for the better, through the value of cultural competence.

After the fall of the Berlin Wall in the late 1980s, the world celebrated a new era in commerce, along with the soon-to-follow exponential increase in 1990 of the 1970s start of globalization, enabled through the advent of The World Wide Web. The world was flat again, and cross-border trade skyrocketed in volume, growth, and coinciding profits. Such was the exponential expansion of globalization that the curriculums at business schools globally soon absorbed the principles of scaling into the standard subject matters relating to global business strategy. Multinational organizations grew, in size and number, and all had the same objective in mind – more products for more customers in more parts of the world, for more profit. Concurrently, there has been correlated growth in expatriate workers, professionals residing and working in a country other than their native country. Multinational organizations implemented models of management and control throughout their global expanded organizational structures, appointing company representatives in different global destinations.

More than three decades onward, the business world finds itself confronted with challenges of managing multicultural dimensions prevalent in all three dimensions of a typical organizational transactional pipeline; being upstream/suppliers, instream/staff (human resources), and downstream/customers. These challenges were exacerbated by the COVID-19 pandemic. Organizations were forced to employ work-from-home (WFH) and work-from-anywhere (WFA) practices, multiplying the dimensional challenges of diverse cultures. This was due to expatriate models slowing down, and organizations had to adapt to managing different cultures globally through Cloud connectivity. Physical proximity, needed for building trust between people, was limited. Commerce had to look afresh at how to maintain financial sustainability and competitiveness, globally, working with diverse upstream-, instream- and downstream elements of human diversity.

It is within this context that this book establishes its value and purpose. Just as a Desmond Tutu and a Mohammed Ali changed the world, this book aims to change the way organizations approach strategy by introducing cultural competence as an internal lever of holistic sustainable competitiveness. As business today experiences a potential economically detrimental claw-back in some parts of the world from globalization, and a bleak economic recovery outlook intra- and post-COVID-19, the purpose and value of the book is self-evident. It provides organizations with a different view of how to achieve and maintain holistic competitiveness. It focuses on the uniqueness of cultural competence as an internal strategic competitive differentiator, as opposed to the tried and tested focus areas of external unique selling propositions and product/service differentiators.

Above all, even if not for the sake of increased competitiveness, the reader is provided with practical guidance on how to manage and lead a culturally diverse world of life and work more effectively to the benefit of all.

This book is constructed in eight relatively short and easy-to-read chapters and concludes with an epilogue.

Introduction

Competence refers to the ability to do something successfully. Using Russel Ackoff's Data, Information, Knowledge, and Wisdom (DIKW) Model (Ackoff, 1989) of how we as people learn and develop cognitively, the authors took the late American organizational theorist's model, and positioned the developmental step of understanding between the progressive steps of knowledge, and of wisdom, to better explain cultural competence.

> Russell Lincoln Ackoff (1919–2009) was an American organizational theorist, consultant, and Anheuser-Busch Professor Emeritus of Management Science at the Wharton School, University of Pennsylvania.

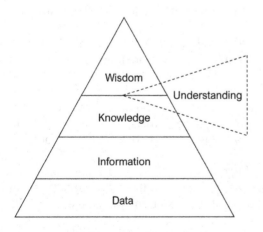

Figure 1.1 Ackoff's Data, Information, Knowledge, and Wisdom Model. Amended. Illustration created by Marina van Zyl.

DOI: 10.4324/9781003303381-1

Amended in this manner, the authors present a kind of a 'mental hierarchy,' containing five steps in the learning and development stages of people. 'Understanding' is a separate step, and the component of learning and development, which improves through the application of what one knows (knowledge). Our level of successful application is measured through the descriptor called 'competence.' The more successful, the more competent. It displays what one knows (knowledge) through a behavioral application. Many, if not most, formal education systems focus on assessing knowledge to determine readiness for progression from one level to another. Be that at school from one grade to the next, or university, from one year to the next. A key difference to prepare people for employment however is experience, hence, the application of knowledge. Knowledge, on its own, is not sufficient. Imagine having to drive a motor vehicle by just studying a manual on how to drive a motor vehicle and passing a written or oral test on the subject matter. One would assume that this is not a preferred method of assessment. Thus, the introduction of understanding is an additional level in our mental hierarchy. Cultural competence, as such, requires the application of culturally competent knowledge constructs in order to improve our understanding thereof.

Why Cultural Competence?

A question many asked of us as authors, as we ventured down the road of authoring this book, was that when there are already so many published materials on cultural intelligence, sensitivity, diversity, respect, and other augmented versions of cultural applicability, why cultural competence? How is cultural competence, specifically, different, and what value can it add to the complex world of managing and leading cultural diversity in our places of work and life?

The answer lies partly in the notion that complexity is better served through diversity than through expertise. But more than that, it lies in what our research uncovered. That cultural competence has the potential of enabling an internal competitive advantage within organizations. This competitive advantage is different from how companies go about creating a point of difference between them and others, focusing on the three variables of a value proposition. These being convenience, affordability, and effectiveness.

Cultural competence is different from that of the traditional external competitive edge that most of us are familiar with – a differentiator situated externally of the organization in the product and/or service delivered to customers.

Such is the nature of this internal competitive advantage that it is more difficult to imitate, compared to the relative ease, at times, with which competing companies typically imitate one another's strategic approaches as well as their products and/or services delivered, resulting in little real differentiation. Of this there are more than enough examples in the world of work, substantiating this point. Both United Parcel Service (UPS) and FedEx, positioned themselves as 'on-time-delivery' competitors in the package delivery race, with only price being a subtle difference between the two. Netflix, as another example, has been joined the streaming industry by competitors like Amazon Prime, and Disney, losing its once-held singular uniqueness of live streaming entertainment. Costa, Starbucks, and Caffe Nero, all offer a coffee experience. Even internationally established brands such as Coca-Cola and Pepsi, McDonalds, and Burger King, suffer the same fate. Arguably, there is a difference in taste, but how many say no to a Pepsi when asking for a Coca-Cola, or vice versa? Who among us drives an extra distance to get to McDonalds, if there is a Burger King closer by? Very few, our research tells us. Why? Well, because they are not particularly different. And so, the list goes on.

Organizations need something different, something completely new to enable sustained holistic competitiveness.

As such, cultural competence does not only focus on how to better leverage diversity in an organization but changes the DNA of an organization in how it behaves; becoming not just the preferred supplier of products/services, but also the preferred place to work. In this book, this behavior refers to how organizations deal with other human systems that constitute the complete transactional pipeline of a commercial cycle. These include, amongst others, the stakeholder components of buyer and seller in Porter's Five Forces (Porter, 2008).

Michael Eugene Porter is an American academic known for his theories on economics, business strategy, and social causes. He is the Bishop William Lawrence University Professor at Harvard Business School. He is the creator of Porter's Five Forces, a framework addressing forces that can be used to guide business strategy to increase competitive advantage.

What Is the Porter's Five Forces Framework

It is a method of analysing the operating environment of a competitor business. It draws from industrial organization economics to derive five forces that determine the competitive intensity and, therefore, the attractiveness (or lack thereof) of an industry in terms of its profitability. An "unattractive" industry is one in which the effect of these five forces reduces overall profitability. The five-forces perspective is associated with its originator, Michael E. Porter of Harvard University, and was first published in *Harvard Business Review* in 1979.

Porter refers to these forces as the micro-environment, to contrast it with the more general term macro-environment, represented through the PEST acronym explained below. The five forces include three forces from 'horizontal competition' – the threat of substitute products or services, the threat of established rivals, and the threat of new entrants – and two others from 'vertical' competition – the bargaining power of suppliers and the bargaining power of customers.

A change in any of the forces normally requires an organization to re-assess the marketplace given the overall change in industry information.

Porter developed his five forces framework in reaction to the then-popular SWOT analysis, also explained below, which he found lacking in rigor.

Positioning Porter's Five Forces within the authors' understanding of Ackoff's model (cf. Figure 1.1), organizations primarily use Porter's Five Forces to gather data for purposes of increasing the informational context and content of the competitive landscape within which they compete. Positioning Five Forces as a separate activity within the process of strategic planning; it forms part of the first phase of strategy selection and formulation, which is that of scanning the business environment for data collection purposes. The steps followed are scenario planning, strategy selection, and execution.

Some organizations also use Porter's model in conjunction with the late Albert S. Humphrey's Strengths, Weaknesses, Opportunities and Threats (SWOT) (Helms & Nixon, 2010). The model was originally created in the 1960s. Organizations also combine Francis Joseph Aguilar's model of Politics, Economy, Social trend changes, Technology (PEST) (Aguilar, 1967) when performing business environmental analysis. PEST was created in 1967.

Albert S. Humphrey was an American business and management consultant who specialized in organizational management and cultural change. Initially earning degrees in chemical engineering in Illinois, he eventually moved to London.

Francis Joseph Aguilar (August 19, 1932–February 17, 2013) was an American scholar of strategic planning and general management. He joined the faculty of Harvard Business School in 1964 and became a tenured professor there in 1971.

What Is PEST Analysis?

PEST Analysis (political, economic, social, and technological) is a management method whereby an organization can assess major external factors that influence its operation in order to become more competitive in the market. As described by the acronym, those four areas are central to this model. A variation on the PEST Analysis format is the PESTLE strategic planning approach, which includes the additional aspects of Legal and Environmental. It is believed that PEST Analysis was first introduced under the name ETPS by Harvard professor Francis J. Aguilar. In the 1967 publication "Scanning the Business Environment," Aguilar presented the economic, technical, political, and social factors as being major influences on the business environment. Subsequently, the letters were rearranged to create a convenient and quirky acronym used today. Generally, it is more effective with larger organizations that are more likely to experience the effects of macro events. PEST analysis is commonly used in conjunction with SWOT analysis, which stands for strengths, weaknesses, opportunities, and threats.

What Is SWOT Analysis?

A SWOT analysis is a compilation of an organization's Strengths, Weaknesses, Opportunities and Threats. The primary objective of a SWOT analysis is to help organizations develop a full awareness of all the factors involved in making a business decision. A SWOT analysis precedes resource allocation in an organization, whether exploring new initiatives, revamping internal policies, considering opportunities to pivot, or altering a plan midway through its execution. A SWOT analysis is used to discover recommendations and strategies, with a focus on leveraging strengths and opportunities to overcome weaknesses and threats.

These models have evolved over time, but by and large, are still being used in this format, for purposes of data gathering.

These models are used to envision a coherent and complete representation of the business environment in which organizations compete. This informational component of the competitive landscape increases the knowledge an organization has thereof. As such, it guides appropriate strategic decisions to achieve sustainable growth and holistic competitiveness.

Cultural competence has a particular impact on the way in which the stakeholder, buyer, and seller components in Porter's model, are managed. The components that make up the model: Buyer; Supplier; Substitute Products; New Entrants; and Existing Rivalry; provide a structured way within which to gather information from the competitive environment. It should be thus appreciated that cultural competence focuses on *how* to manage the human dynamics embedded in these components. More specifically, buyers, suppliers, staff (internal human resources), and related stakeholders. This management and behavior bring about the emergence of an organizational cultural and behavioral DNA, a way of application, which can become its internal competitive advantage if institutionalized correctly.

Through the unfolding narrative of the chapters of this book, the recipe of how to identify, develop, and enable such an internal competitive advantage, is explained.

Chapter Breakdown

For ease of reading, Chapters One to Four have been grouped and themed together as the 'what,' 'how,' and 'where' of cultural competence. Chapter One explains what cultural competence is. Chapter Two tells us how it is embedded in the culture of an organization, focusing on the *culture* part in cultural competence. Chapter Three explains how to integrate it into the Strategy Planning Processes and into the values of the organization. Chapter Four adds to Chapters Two and Three, by elaborating on the need for having a learner-mindset as a prerequisite thought paradigm when wanting to establish cultural competence as a dominating organizational culture. It does so by reflecting on the Satya Nadella case study as leader of Microsoft, at the time of authoring this book. Chapter Four ends with the question of whether cultural competence can be measured and improved, as it leads into Chapter Five and the remaining chapters in the book.

Chapter One

This Chapter explains what cultural competence is by providing more detail on how it differs from cultural interest, awareness, understanding, sensitivity, and intelligence. Defined clearly, the authors refer to cultural competence as a drop of ink in a glass of water, impacting the entire organizational DNA and bringing forth an emergent internal competitive advantage.

Chapter Two

Chapter Two positions cultural competence as the enabler of a difficult-to-imitate, internal competitive advantage, within an organization's practices of dealing with the upstream, instream, and downstream human elements (Porter's Five Forces) of a typical transactional pipeline. This enabling component focuses on the imperative of cultural competence as a key ingredient of strategy. The chapter highlights the strategic value of cultural competence at a time when the center of innovation, aimed at sustained competitiveness, evolved from business model-centric innovation (capturing value) to platform-centric innovation (creating value) and ultimately to experience-centric innovation (delivering value).

Chapter Three

Whereas Chapter Two describes a compelling argument toward the strategic value of cultural competence; Chapter Three shows the reader how to integrate cultural competence into the organizations' strategy planning process(es). In doing so, it elaborates on the notion started in Chapter Two, that cultural competence differs significantly as an internal competitive advantage, compared to one retained in product and/or service differentiation only. As such, the chapter illustrates how to ensure that cultural competence is structurally considered at every strategy planning step/stage, informing its outcome.

Chapter Four

Having a clear understanding of what cultural competence is, how it gives emergence to an internal competitive advantage, and having a recipe for integrating it into the strategy planning process(es) of an organization; Chapter Four guides the reader in how to embed cultural competence into the values system of the organization, making it part of the fabric of the organization. This is of particular importance as this is the part making it difficult for competitors to imitate, making it possible to extend a lead in the challenge of remaining sustainably competitive. Uniqueness and differentiation evolve from an external focus on product and/or service offerings to the internal DNA of organizations. The chapter closes the loop on the narrative started in Chapter Two on how cultural competence can become a strategic imperative in bringing about a new alternative, difficult to imitate, organizational strength.

At this point, the reader might wonder how cultural competence as an organizational culture is any different to culture in general. There is indeed an abundance of research and practice that lay testimony to the importance of culture in an organization as it grounds organizational behavior. The question arises of what is the difference. Is cultural competence not just another angle or a play on the importance of culture in general? The subsequent chapters aim to address this question.

Chapter Five

Chapter Five illustrates its value by focusing on the competence part of its definition, more than the cultural part. This is detailed through a measuring matrix, measuring what the authors term 'The Cultural Competence Index (CCI);' which determines an organization's cultural competence performance. In this way, an organization can get an indication of its own level of performance related to cultural competence and consider exploring the correlation between higher levels of cultural competence performance and increased holistic competitive sustainability of an organization.

From the outset of explaining the value of cultural competence, it is positioned and contextualized within three separate frameworks, explained in full later in the book. These frameworks include a framework for strategic decision-making, Porter's Five Forces, and a framework through which we view the organization as a system. In the case of Porter's Five Forces framework, the authors consider the upstream, instream, and downstream stakeholders involved in the CCI. These are customers/buyers (downstream), staff (instream), and suppliers (upstream). The CCI also includes stakeholders such as government and regulatory bodies, which is contained in Porter's Five (and a Half) Forces; as well as host country partnering (existing rivalry), for which the authors consulted work on Hofstede's entry modes. These models are elaborated on in further chapters of this book. Competence, in cultural competence, is measured through the CCI by determining the contribution that cultural competence makes in the success achieved, or not, in an organization's performance.

Chapter Six

Chapter Six expands on the explanation of the CCI composition by providing case study examples on each of the variables and constructs comprising the CCI. This includes the human dimension (soft skills component) of Porter's Five Forces, specifically that of suppliers, buyers, and other external stakeholders. The other variables and constructs are taken from frameworks that include employees, governance, and human resource support. Thus, whereas Chapter Five provides a conceptual explanation of the composition of the CCI, Chapter Six provides case study examples of the use of the CCI.

Chapter Seven

Chapter Seven builds directly on Chapter Six and shows the reader how to implement the CCI within an organization: enabling continuous measurement of its cultural competence contribution to holistic sustained competitiveness. Tips and guidance on improving the real-time cultural competence performance of an organization are provided and critical success factors are identified to ensure continuous improvement. The chapter focuses on institutionalizing cultural competence. For this to happen, the change required for the successful institutionalization of cultural competence needs to be programmed into an organization's wider systemic method of operations, internally of, and externally to, the organization. The chapter refers to both Kanter's Change Wheel and Kotter's Eight-Step processes of change as it provides a step-by-step method for institutionalizing cultural competence through a change management framework; becoming the "drop of ink" in a glass of water, as referred to in Chapter One.

Chapter Eight

Having completed the narrative on cultural competence as an internal strength, ensuring longer-term sustainable competitiveness, Chapter Eight describes future challenges and opportunities for cultural competence. It explores some future challenges on the horizon with reference to the age of digitization, artificial intelligence, connectedness, distributed work-force, virtual management, virtual teams, and other exciting developments heading our way; all related to the importance of embracing cultural competence as an internal strategic differentiator.

The Epilogue

The epilogue summarizes the key points of the preceding chapters, as a final overview of the value of the CCI in enabling holistic sustained competitiveness in organizations.

Cultural Competence
A Drop of Ink in a Glass of Water

Introduction

To fully understand the meaning of cultural competence and its strategic competitive value, this chapter explains how cultural competence should be viewed and approached as a type of progression in understanding the different augmented definitions which all incorporate a cultural element. Henceforth the authors compare it with synoptic explanations of other references to culture when looking for ways to improve all performance through the discipline of managing, leading, and optimizing diversity, across the entire transactional pipeline (up-, in-, and downstream). In practice, and in literature, there are numerous references to cultural interest, awareness, understanding, sensitivity, and intelligence. To understand how cultural competence differs from these, the authors take a brief look at them for purposes of clarity through comparison.

The Systemic Impact of Cultural Competence as an Invention

The authors explain cultural competence through the metaphor of a drop of ink in a glass of water. This explanation is best achieved through the paradigm of viewing cultural competence systemically as an invention (to invent something) of sorts.

So, why Invention?

As systems thinkers, it is the view of the authors that invention itself holds little value unless it can be incorporated into a larger system and contribute to increased systemic value. As an example, the authors share the viewpoint that the true genius of someone like Thomas Edison, did not rely on his ability to invent alone. The true genius, and for that matter, true value, was his ability to conceive complete systems. The authors support this view as they consider whether the invention of the lightbulb would

DOI: 10.4324/9781003303381-2

have been so life-changing had it not been part of a larger system. The same can be said for other life-changing inventions, from sewers of ancient Rome around 500BC, to the invention of the micro-processor. The moment an invention contributes to systemic value, like Edison's lightbulb contributed to the facilitation of changing the social and economic structure of society, such an invention is seen as systemically valuable, like a drop of ink in a glass of water. It literally changes everything, in this case, for the better.

The authors view cultural competence as a systemic invention that alters the DNA of the organization. It is altered in such a way that not only do organizations differentiate themselves from the competition but it does so through the creation of a unique internal competitive advantage. This internal nature of competitive advantage makes it difficult to imitate by competitors. In the book, the authors explain why and how managing such an invention properly can greatly assist in achieving holistic sustainable competitiveness for organizations.

Readers may well ask why cultural competence is regarded as an invention. Why not just an initiative or change management project – is it all that new? There is also the difference between culture and civilization to be considered as the authors aim to rule out any ambiguity at this stage. Culture, as applied here, is the term used by the authors to denote the manifestation of the manner in which humans think, behave, and act. Civilization on the other hand, refers to the process through which a region, or society, out-stretches advanced stages of human- and societal development.

The Answer to Why Cultural Competence Is Viewed as an Invention, Is Two-Fold

Firstly, it needs to be said that many organizations apply scale and scope of economies to pursue financial sustainability through increased profits. At the turn of the previous century, business model flexibility, whereby organizations reconfigured the application of their assets and resources (going lean), was common amongst most organizations to increase profitability. As technical (tech) companies grew over time, platform-centric innovations became more popular and saw a rise in scalability practices. Today, it is fairly common for organizations to have a platform business model, be that as complement, substitute, or disruptor of their existing business model. Many companies are focusing on experience-centric innovations, leveraging technology to enhance customer experience through value delivery and pursue scale to increase profitability.

However, the approach of scalability is not new, just exponentially enhanced through technology. Scalability has worked well since the 1980s, the same time that many international business schools adopted this principle into the global business strategy curricula. The content of such curricula included teaching methods of opportunistic exploitation of the differences in global labor and associated costs. In today's multi-cultural workforce and market compositions, this approach is sometimes frowned upon as there are those who argue that it had led to an unbalanced fragile economy, globally. Globalization is also partially blamed for this fragility, as not everyone seemed to have benefitted by its growth. Few phenomena illustrated this economic fragility, which coincides with these methodologies of scaling costs through global exploitation, as well as that of the economic destruction caused by the Covid-19 pandemic. It is this model of financial competitiveness and sustainability, driven primarily by a profit motive through the reduction of costs, which led to large-scale single sourcing of products, from primarily one part of the world. The same part of the world, it so happened to be, where COVID-19 virus was first reported as to have been detected.

As the international manufacturing powerhouse of the globe, China had to shut down through lockdowns and other strict measures taken to suppress the spread of the deadly virus.

> The Covid-19 virus is widely believed to have originated in the sprawling capital of Central China's Hubei province, Wuhan. It is a commercial center divided by the Chang Jiang and Han rivers in the larger South-Eastern part of China.

Thus, because of the drive of low-cost manufacturing, a principle of a scalability model to increase profitability, many globally trading companies were left with inventory shortfalls when China locked down. But China alone cannot be blamed for this. Partial blame also needs to go to global trading companies' lack of diversification through contingent supply lines. A shortsighted, probably profit-only driven, strategic error. The global ramifications were horrific. Intra- and post-pandemic, because of this fragility experienced in our economic system(s), organizations are today seeking different approaches that are more robust and resilient towards potential future disruptions.

It is on the back of this seeking of different approaches by business leaders, and consumers who were left without products of various sorts (commodities or consumables), that the authors argue in favor of an internal strategic differentiator. The aim of which would be to replace the 'me-too' and 'same-old-same-old' methodologies of achieving competitive holistic sustainability through scale and scope of economies. Cultural competence may very well be such an alternative different approach.

The above narrative provides content to the argument substantiating the first reason the authors view cultural competence as an invention. It is something new, something different, and has a systemic impact in the change related to conventional sustained competitiveness.

The second part of the two-fold answer, provided to the question of why the authors view cultural competence as an invention, lies in the difference between cultural competence and that of cultural awareness, knowledge, sensitivity, and intelligence. This is further explained in the next section, how cultural competence differs from cultural interest, awareness, understanding, sensitivity, and intelligence.

Cultural Interest

Cultural interest refers to people relating to specific aspects of cultures other than their own. This relation might be through other interests, like that of one's heritage. A South African, as an example, from European decent might have a particular interest in European history and culture as the individual might feel related to it, to a more or lesser extent. People also may have particular pursuits of cultural events or artistic displays in different forms exhibited by diverse cultures.

Cultural Awareness

Cultural awareness, on the other hand, is primarily associated with a level of understanding the differences between nationalities and cultures. It can also, however, include cultural differences within one nation. Whether that is amongst the multicultural population categories in China for instance, or the diverse indigenous cultures in a country like South Africa where cultural differences exist between the Zulu and Xhosa Indigenous ethnic groups, despite their shared origin. These differences are observed in the attitudes, behaviors, and values of people from different countries, backgrounds, and belief systems. However, this awareness alone is not enough for organizations to leverage the internal values and belief systems of a multicultural workforce for strategic- and operational competitiveness. For this, a level of cultural understanding is required.

Cultural Understanding

Cultural understanding is elevating awareness of culture to an attempt of comprehending it, specifically for purposes of building cross-cultural relationships and optimizing the strength in that. This is necessary if one person wants to understand the views, values, humor, hopes, loyalties, worries and fears of another person, or persons, from a different culture and not to judge over it.

Cultural knowledge and understanding helps one in shaping a unique perspective on matters, framed through the cultural lens of someone else's different, culturally informed, view. In a way, this relates to cultural sensitivity, whereby the awareness of cultural differences and similarities between people is understood and biases are removed. This is applicable in cases of categorizing diverse cultures without dividing them into right and/or wrong, better, and/or worse.

Cultural Intelligence

In the final instance, organizations refer to cultural intelligence, based on the world-renowned research done by the late Geert Hofstede (Alves et al., 2006), when considering entry mode options in cases of expanding business interests and operations into another (host) country.

It denotes an individual's ability to collaborate successfully with people from diverse cultural backgrounds, in pursuing common interest and shared expectations from a global organization. It is something most people can relate to as it refers to 'getting along' with others, to a greater or lesser extent. An individual's cultural intelligence is what enables him/her to communicate, collaborate, and negotiate in the business world with those from diverse cultural backgrounds. These are all key skills and abilities needed to enable organizations in pursuit of internationalizing their business interests and operations to be successful in global markets. Cultural intelligence, as a science and methodology of selecting the right entry mode into other parts of the world through joint ventures, partnership, mergers, and acquisitions, is best known through the work that Hofstede researched and produced on it.

Gerard Hendrik Hofstede was a Dutch social psychologist, IBM employee, and Professor Emeritus of Organizational Anthropology and International Management at Maastricht University in the Netherlands, well known for his pioneering research on cross-cultural groups and organizations.

A host country as he explains it, is a country where a company, which is based in another country, has business activities.

The entry mode refers to the selection of a specific business model choice to break into a host country's market (Tams & Arthur, 2007).

Additional to Hofstede's framework of entry mode selection, the nature of the contextual and transactional composition of the host country's competitive landscape is considered. This is done through various tools of analysis, one which the authors have made frequent reference to already in this book, Porter's Five Forces. Porter's model is used to shape the host country's competitive landscape, informing an organization's specific entry mode (joint ventures, partnership, mergers, and acquisitions, other) to be selected for a higher probability of competitive success in that region.

What Is Cultural Competence then?

Cultural competence is the successful application of cultural interests, awareness, understanding, sensitivity, and intelligence. In the context of this book, cultural competence is viewed as an ingredient to create an internal competitive edge, difficult to imitate.

A way to illustrate and distinguish between cultural intelligence and competence is to reference Ackoff's mental hierarchy of learning, cited in the introductory chapter of this book.

According to Ackoff, people progress through stages of learning as they develop in life. The lowest level of learning refers to raw data. For example, one sees, observes, and takes note of a road sign. Using this raw data and processing it so that a person knows what it means provides one with information. People now know that this sign with numbers and different colors on it indicates the speed limit on a country's roads. Processing this information; it provides people with knowledge that the speed limit should not be exceeded.

As mentioned in the introductory chapter, the authors added/inserted the level of understanding in the DIKW model to complement Ackoff's model and contribute to the mental hierarchy of learning. Knowing that one should not exceed the speed limit is one thing but knowing why not, is another. At this level, a person understands that transgressing the limit is dangerous, could lead to accidents, a traffic fine, and so on. The implication of wrongful behavior is considered and understood.

The pinnacle of the mental hierarchy is wisdom. In life, some people learn through their mistakes, as much as what they celebrate and learn from success. It is the wrong turns in life that, in time, ends up being the stepping-stones of our development to achieve success. In 2013 Chief Executive Officer Ron Johnson from former JC Penny fame in America, recollected the mistakes he made in contributing to the share price devaluation at JC Penny (Narayandas, Margolis, & Raffaelli, 2017).

Ron Johnson is the CEO and founder of Enjoy Technology. Previously, he was the senior vice president of retail operations at Apple Inc., where he pioneered the concept of the Apple Retail Stores and the Genius Bar, and the vice president of merchandising for Target Corporation, where he was credited for making the store appeal to a younger and trendier crowd.

He beautifully coins the term *situational arrogance;* as he talks to Harvard Business School students about what he learnt from his mistakes. The mistake being that he forgot, for a moment, that the contributors to individual success, other than the individual him or herself, are that of the larger business contextual environment (contextual intelligence) and, the organization or team. Some also argued that the reason for the failure was that Johnson used 'gut,' not 'data,' in making decisions for strategic growth. Interesting, because research done by Anthony J. Mayo and Nitin Nohria indicated that organizational success is more dependent on contextual factors of influence than on a CEO's ability to read the future (Mayo & Nohria, 2005).

Tony Mayo is the Thomas S. Murphy Senior Lecturer of Business Administration and C. Roland Christensen Distinguished Management Educator in the Organizational Behavior Unit of Harvard Business School (HBS).

Nitin Nohria is an Indian American academic. He served as the tenth dean of Harvard Business School. He is also the George F. Baker Professor of Administration. He is also a former non-executive director of Tata Sons.

Or rather, the latter was a distinct leadership trait whereby business leaders would 'read' the context, cited as contextual intelligence.

Learning from mistakes is not new, but it is a skill and requires a willingness by the individual to pursue a growth mindset. A skill fostered through self-reflective or 'experiential' learning. It is through this self-reflective learning that wisdom is acquired, which is the pinnacle in Ackoff's DIKW model.

Cultural Competence and Wisdom

If cultural competence is a type of progression from levels of awareness to levels of competence, one can position it on the level of wisdom, referring to Ackoff's model depicted in Figure 1.1. Cultural competence is not only about knowing facts about other cultures and different cultural behaviors. Differences for instance in how to greet, what to say, where to sit, what to eat, and what not. It is much more than such a 'to-do' or 'not-to-do' list. Understanding cultures and imbuing cultural competency in a business approach has implications and knowing how to harness and leverage these effects can elevate the performance of the organization.

To simplify the explanation, the following example is cited of two people crossing paths from two different cultures. Let us imagine a Moroccan Arabian and a French businessperson, engaging in a project, working side by side, and, to distinguish it from Hofstede's cultural intelligence entry-mode model, it is assumed they are expatriates, working for and in the same organization.

Firstly, cultural awareness would enable them to realize they are from different cultures and therefore display different behaviors in reaction to different phenomena. These might be language, humor, body language and other cultural differences.

Secondly, cultural sensitivity will lead them to respect these differences and not judge or stereotype them. This will be an act of mutual respect.

Thirdly, cultural intelligence will enable them to, despite their cultural and heritage background differences, work together and synergize in some way, through an aligned business model.

Fourthly, cultural competence, however, goes one step further where the individuals start thinking differently about one another's culture.

Thinking differently in the sense that they grow curious and extend an interest to learn from one another. Really getting to know the cultural drivers and values of the other party, not ontologically, but immersing themselves in the other's culture for complete understanding without compromising or 'losing' their own cultural footing. This act of learning from one another is followed by actions taken by the parties involved with the aim of achieving a higher level of success when working with one another, to the benefit of the organization and all its stakeholders, as opposed to not. As such, the authors are of the view that this is beyond a cultural tolerance. It is an embrace of differences that would be valued in terms of essential learning towards gaining greater wisdom!

To complete Ackoff's mental hierarchy explanation, wisdom refers to the process of reflecting on one's understanding and knowing when and how to leverage one's knowledge and understanding. Referring to the example of road signs and driving, wisdom would be exceeding the speed limit in exceptional circumstances, such as medical emergencies, dangerous situations, and others. In other words, it is that moment where a sense of integrity and judgment comes into play, not necessarily scripted by a higher authority like the police or other authorities. Wisdom would be knowing when and how to leverage cultural competence to the organization's greatest advantage.

'A drop of ink... ... .'

If one had to define cultural competence with a typical definition, it would most likely relate to the ability to understand, communicate, and effectively and emphatically interact with people across different cultural backgrounds. However, as indicated in the example of the Moroccan and French businesspersons, practice has taught the authors that it is much more, and hence the authors refer to it as a 'drop of ink' in a glass of water. It is a way of working with others, an attitude, internally and externally, that becomes the culture of the organization and at the same time 'castles' the organization, like in the game of Chess.

In chess, Castling is a move that allows for two pieces to be moved simultaneously. The king moves two spaces to the left or to the right, and the rook moves over and in front of the king, all in one move. In chess, castling places the player's king in a strong defensible position, making it almost impossible for the opposing player to penetrate the defensive wall built around the king when making this move.

It is the significance in what this move accomplishes that makes it an understandable metaphor for the value of cultural competence to an organization. Just as this chess move provides a 'difficult-to-penetrate' strategy in chess, cultural competence provides an organization with a kind of strategic competitiveness, difficult to imitate. It evolves from the notion of resource-based strategic approaches to that of a more intangible competitiveness. It does not use the normal set of differentiators, leverages an internal strength, and is extremely difficult to copy.

It is a way in which to ensure improvement of performance on different variables, enabling the organization with the possibility of constantly outperforming others and remaining holistically sustainable and competitive. It infiltrates the entire organization and embeds itself as a unique behavioral differentiator. It becomes the DNA of the organization which cannot be copied, nor imitated by competitors. It is something that changes how organizations do business and it changes the culture of the organization itself. It does the same thing to organizations as what Claus Schwab said technology does to people/us: 'It does not change how we do things, but it changes us.'

Klaus Martin Schwab is a German engineer, economist, and founder of the World Economic Forum (WEF). He has acted as the WEF's chairperson since founding the organization in 1971.

Chapter One: Key Take-aways

- Cultural competence should be viewed as an invention, something that has a systemic impact on the organization.
- The strategic focus of cost reduction to increase margin and profitability has yielded a fragile global economic system over time.
- Cultural competence can replace the 'same-old-same-old' strategic approaches of cost (willingness to sell) and value add (willingness to pay) by focusing on an internal differentiator as opposed to an external product/service differentiator.
- Cultural competence can be equated to levels of understanding and wisdom in Ackoff's amended mental hierarchy of how we learn and develop, distinguishing itself from other descriptions of cultural diversity and focusing on the ability to apply what one knows about cultural diversity.
- Cultural competence 'castles' an organization, providing it with an internal strategic advantage, yielding organizational competitiveness that is difficult to copy or imitate.

The Imperativeness of Culture in Cultural Competence

Introduction

More than a decade ago, before having to deal with the exponential complexities of a worldwide post- and intra-COVID-19 pandemic; one of the authors found himself flying back from Sudan. This was after a two-year consulting contract in Khartoum, the capital of what was once a unified Sudan. He thought back on passing over Mount Kilimanjaro and the jaw-dropping view it offered. Sipping coffee in the relative comfort of his seat, he admired the sun's rays scraping the mountaintop, leaving it breathtakingly silver as the gale force winds pushed the top layer of snow into the horizon.

Returning to South Africa after a challenging two-year acting CEO position, he remembered how he could not help, but to be mesmerized by the simple beauty of the mountainscape as he marveled at the sight of nature below. However, fresh reflection from the time in Khartoum hijacked his thoughts of simplicity and he could not help but to ponder over how challenging it had become for some organizations to remain holistically competitive during those times. If only it was as simple on the ground as what it appeared to be from the sky, but it was not. As one descends from the skies, one must face the complex business world full of multi-dimensional challenges, regulations, customer needs, competition, and more.

After Sudan became independent, the Jaafar Nimeiry regime began Islamist rule. This exacerbated the rift between the Islamic North, the seat of the government, and the Animists and Christians in the South. Differences in ethnicity, language, religion, and political power erupted in a civil war between government forces, influenced by the National Islamic Front (NIF), and the southern rebels, whose most influential faction was the Sudan People's Liberation Army (SPLA), which eventually led to the independence of South Sudan in 2011.

DOI: 10.4324/9781003303381-3

Even as far back in 2010, not only did organizations have to deal with the increased multi-dimensionality of workforce and customers, but they also faced the challenges of an increased velocity and intensity of business environmental changes, exacerbated by the rise of Tech companies. Today, it is even more the case as competitiveness has become exponentially much more complex in the recent past, compared to before. And, truth be told, not just for multinationals who chose a strategy of internationalization and globalization, but for any business that must draw on global skills, suppliers, expertise, and the likes, to get the job done.

From the explanation offered in Chapter One, it is clear what is meant by cultural competence and how this differs from related associations to culture. In this chapter, the authors deepen the explanation of the application of cultural competence in the world of business. The authors explain the application thereof by focusing on the imperativeness of *culture*, in the term, cultural competence. The chapter includes a discussion on how cultural competence, as a differentiator and enabler of sustained holistic competitiveness, differs from that of end-product and/or service differentiation. In doing so, the authors introduce an alternative view, approach, and understanding, for sustained holistic competitiveness, introduced during Chapter One. This alternative is compared to that of well-known taught and implemented model(s) of exploiting the scale and scope of economies, especially through global expansion strategies, also mentioned in Chapter One. It can be argued that it is because of these practices that organizations do not necessarily leverage an internal strength as a competitive edge. Multinationals, in particular, diversify the application of their resources and take advantage of imbalances in international labor practices and the associated costs. Diversifying their operations might even extend to include raw material sourcing and the functioning – or malfunctioning – of regional and global capital markets.

However, from the research in which the authors measured recent- and current successes of global multinationals, they observe a different trend. The trend leads to questioning the so-called guarantees of these resource-based strategic approaches toward financial sustainability and competitiveness. This critical view on tried and tested strategic approaches are primarily brought about by the complexities created when cause and consequence (causality) are not as visible in a chaotic, disrupted, and, complex state, as what they are in a simpler environment. To elaborate on this statement for the reason(s) of organizations taking a more critical view of known strategic approaches, it is helpful to contextualize this argument within the framework of Porter's Five Forces, often mentioned in Chapter One. More particularly, it is necessary to differentiate between hard and soft skills components embedded in Porter's model.

The origin of the term 'soft skills' can be traced back to the US Military between 1968 and 1972. The military had excelled at training troops in how to use machines to do their job. But they were noticing that a lot of what made a group of soldiers victorious was not machine related but rather how the group was led. One skill was to use a map for instance (hard skill), and it was another explaining how to use a map, motivate others to use it, be accountable and take decisions on an empowered level (soft skills), based on reading a map.

Organizations understand the hard skills part of Porter's Five Forces, but do they understand the soft skills part and how cultural competence fits into all of this? What is meant by this, and what is this assumed relation between cultural competence, and Porter's Five Forces?

Cultural Competence and Porter's Five Forces

Through their research, the authors stumbled upon an interesting phenomenon when it comes to applying the Five Forces model. It was found that the effectiveness of performing a Porter's Five Forces analysis appears to rely more on soft skills, than hard skills, for its relevance, value, applicability, and contribution to organizational competitiveness. The hard skills component refers to the ability to analyze existing rivalry, barriers to entry, suppliers, buyers, substitute products, and new entrants, through a T-bone (horizontal and vertical) deep dive analysis, typical analytical thinking. However, whereas such an analysis would reveal the content reality of each component, it is the management of the respective stakeholder components in the framework (suppliers and buyers, and even government in the case of Porter's Five – (and a Half) – Forces model), that enables organizations to raise the barrier to entry and increase their chances of holistic sustainable competitiveness.

Porter lists the government as a "Factor," not a force, along with subordinate variables like the industry growth rate and complementary products and services. Porter argues that government is not best understood as a sixth force because government involvement is neither inherently good nor bad for industry profitability. The best way to understand the influence of government on competition is to analyze how specific government policies affect the five competitive forces. For instance, patents raise barriers to entry, boosting industry profit potential. Conversely, government policies favoring unions may raise supplier power and diminish profit potential. Government operates at multiple levels and through many different policies, each of which will affect the structure in different ways.

The management of stakeholders refers specifically to how organizations, the people in organizations, build and manage relations with people representing the stakeholder components. It became apparent through the research that in a globalized business landscape, cultural competence is an imperative for organizations wanting to 'get it right' when expanding their business through the influence of people who happen to be from different cultures.

The same can be said about relationships when people share the same culture. However, things tend to be a bit trickier when different cultural backgrounds collide in a working relationship. Be that as Suppliers, Joint Venture parties in a host country as explained by Hofstede, buyers, government officials, or any other transactional stakeholder necessary for operational ability.

Figure 2.1 contextualizes this soft skills element and refers to it as the Cultural Competence Realm, represented in the figure by the two-way grey arrows. Organizations can, as such, castle (cf. Chapter One) themselves by exercising cultural competence in dealing with the human systems embedded in Porter's model. Strategizing relative to suppliers, buyers, government, and others, involves dealing with people, by default, hence, human systems. If done in a culturally competent way, dealing

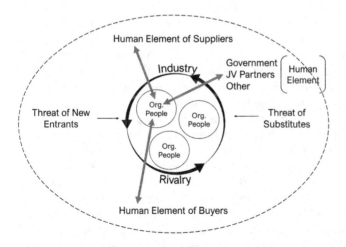

Figure 2.1 The Cultural Competence Realm: Amended (Porter, 2008). Illustration created by Marina van Zyl.

with stakeholders embedded in Porter's model, an internal competitive advantage is created – castling.

In this chapter, the authors venture into exploring cultural competence as an intangible core competency contributing to the holistic sustainable competitiveness of organizations. This core competency is proving to be much more of a competitive differentiator than that of mere smarter resource application diversification between organizations, both on a strategic and operational level. It leans more toward soft skill ability than hard skill qualification and expertise, which closes the loop on the authors' argument that to achieve cultural competence, Porter's model is more dependent on soft skills ability than that of hard skills.

Note: Buyers, as termed in the Cultural Competence Realm refer to a business-to-business (B-B) transactional model. In the case of a business-to-customer (B-C) transactional model, the authors refer to customer in the case of products, and to client, in the case of services.

Strategy and the Strive for Uniqueness

The growth of multinational and multicultural organizations, both in size and number, resulted in very few of them still competing with local competitors confined to a single geographical region – be that state, country, or region. Pictures of intergalactic giants, such as those from the Transporter movies, come to mind when thinking of these large multinational conglomerates! In fact, multinationals are increasingly competing with one another directly, 'many of them, as found through the authors' research, still with similar capabilities and strategic approaches to sustainable competitiveness. These similarities refer to the scale and scope of economies, internationalization of production and manufacturing workforces, making use of capital market differences, and, to some extent, government, and regional trade block incentives.

With level playing fields and increased players joining, organizations are forced to dig deeper and take a fresh look at internal core competencies as possible differentiators that they can leverage over their competitors, as opposed to those linked to resource application diversification. The strategic competitive value lies in breaking with the norm and not using the same set of differentiators. The authors' research shows that there is a need to leverage an internal uniqueness that should be difficult for competition to copy and/or imitate, which is one of the critical aims of strategy and its product and/or service output. This key aim of the strategy is becoming increasingly difficult as strategy is limited in its options of pursuing holistic competitiveness. The research indicates that in cases where profit-centric competitiveness is pursued, there are standard approaches followed by many organizations in this pursuit, also related to competitive success. These are, amongst others, 'willingness to buy,' and/or 'willingness to sell.'

The following explanation on the difference between these approaches is to be noted, as the authors prepare to argue why the *culture*, in cultural competence, is so important to provide an alternative to external cost and/or differentiation offerings.

Generic Profit-Centric Approaches

Figure 2.2 illustrates this difference.

The research indicates that many organizations understand the notion of *value capturing*, whereby an organization will have a baseline cost with an added margin (mark-up) to determine the price that a product and/or service is offered at. Beyond this, *value creation* refers to an innovative focus, targeting areas of additional customer value-add as well as areas of cost-saving initiatives. These cost-saving initiatives are not based on a model of exploitation, but on a model of mutual benefit, whereby the cost-reduction benefits are shared between the organization initiating the cost-reduction drive, and the supplier implementing it. An example would be

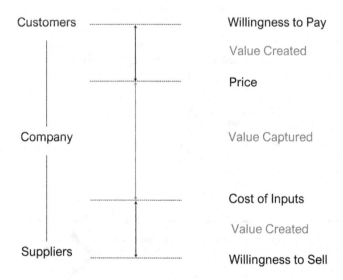

Figure 2.2 Different Profit-Centric Strategy Approaches: Amended (Oberholzer-Gee, 2021). Illustration created by Marina van Zyl.

the initiatives whereby Walmart invests in systems resulting in a cost saving to their suppliers, and then share the benefits thereof, mutually.

> Walmart Inc. is an American multinational retail corporation that operates a chain of hypermarkets, discount department stores, and grocery stores from the United States, headquartered in Bentonville, Arkansas.

In pursuing the strategic approach of value creation, organizations stretch the return on capital invested through increased price points (willingness to buy) and/or reduced cost (willingness to sell).

Evolved Customer-Centric Approaches

An additional dimension yielded through the research, generating prominence during the COVID-19 pandemic, is that of *value delivery*. This is illustrated in Figure 2.3.

Referencing to Figure 2.2, note the approaches of value capturing and value-creating, similarly used in Figure 2.3 as an output of a chosen approach. What the authors add here in Figure 2.3 is an evolved approach that focuses on value delivery, visible on the right-hand side of Figure 2.3. Most organizations know business model-centric innovation and consider it as part of an optimization of assets model. 'Going lean,' is the most used term when referring to this type of approach. Coupled with this, the advent of technical-orientated companies/organizations have over time exploited and explored existing assets configuration and resource application aiming at achieving platform-centric opportunities, which focuses on value creation.

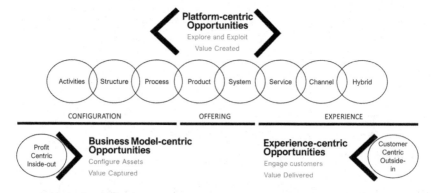

Figure 2.3 Strategic Approach beyond Standard Approaches. Illustration created by Marina van Zyl.

In these instances, organizations reinvent and/or recombine capabilities to create value.

The focus for value creation is primarily on exploiting and exploring existing and augmented products, and system delivery, as indicated in Figure 2.3, under platform-centric opportunities. In turn, business-model-centric innovation focuses more on activities, structure, and process. Both these approaches tend to lean more toward a profit-centric driven approach, versus experience-centric opportunities – the latter being a more customer-centric approach.

As illustrated in Figure 2.3, experience-centric innovation focuses on the service, channel, and hybrid components of an evolved business model. It is the latter of these three approaches that the authors associate more freely with, when it comes to the differentiating impact of cultural competence. The reason being that this evolved model is predominantly more customer/people-focused. This is mainly due to the shift organizations make from an 'inside-out' innovation approach to an 'outside-in' innovation approach. In the first approach, organizations have a culturally incompetent view of 'we make, you take.' In the second approach, deep insights are gathered through a process of immersion in the customers-, and other stakeholders in the transactional pipeline's, life. Critical questions are asked pertaining to:

- What problems organizations are trying to solve for their stakeholders?
- What do they think their stakeholders need?
- What are their stakeholders' "pain" points?
- What jobs do their stakeholders need to do?
- What do they think their stakeholders want to accomplish?

This immersion requires a high degree of cultural competence and, if applied correctly, can lead to a much stronger relational status with stakeholders, as opposed to a transactional one. From the authors' research, it is clear that many organizations understand, and are remarkably successful at, capturing and creating value (cf. Figure 2.2), as these are mainly concerned with business-model-centric opportunities and platform-centric opportunities. Delivering value, however, requires a deep-centered connection with stakeholders, for which cultural competence is a key requirement and is needed to explore- and exploit experience-centric opportunities.

A keyword to take cognizance of in Figure 2.3's graphical depiction of this evolvement from configuration, to offering, to experience, is, *engage*. Previously in Porter's Five (and a Half) Forces motif depicted in Figure 2.1, the authors highlighted the down-, up-, and instream components of an organizational transactional pipeline. For the evolved experience-centric opportunities, however, which enable value delivery, organizations require more than business model-centric improvements and platform-centric optimizations. Experience-centric opportunities span beyond the transactional deliverables between customer and organization, even beyond the transactional systems of suppliers and others mentioned in Porter's model. As such, cultural competence emerges more predominantly as an imperative that enables holistic sustainability through focusing on customer engagement and experience. It is at this point where the authors want to position the importance and role of cultural competence, specifically focusing on the culture part of it.

"Culture Eats Strategy for Breakfast"

There is a famous quote from the late Peter Drucker, that says, "culture eats strategy for breakfast."

This implies that the culture of an organization impacts stronger toward its success or failure, regardless of the strategy. As explained through the motifs of Figures 2.2 and 2.3, organizations have the option of increasing profitability by focusing on the willingness-to-buy/sell approach and/or that of the value delivery approach.

> The late Peter Ferdinand Drucker was an Austrian American management consultant, educator, and author, whose writings contributed to the philosophical and practical foundations of the modern business corporation.

This refers to ways and means of adding value and increasing a positive customer experience. This in turn creates a willingness of customers to pay a premium as well as remain loyal, thus increasing the profit margin. Of course, profitability can also be increased organically through scoping economies of more customers through increased market share and internationalization of markets.

With strategic options limited, businesses are struggling to remain holistically sustainable and competitive as they struggle to remain uniquely different. Examples of UPS and FedEx, Coca-Cola and Pepsi, McDonalds, and Burger King, earlier, support this notion. The ability to create and foster something that is difficult for competitors to imitate normally refers to a product and/or service. In most cases though, the competition catches up with technological and/or innovative advantages in just a matter of time. Even Netflix's remarkable disruption of the video rental industry during the earlier decades of this century are now being marred by Amazon Prime, Disney Plus, and others. This proves the point of difficulty in maintaining holistic sustainable competitiveness and the need for an alternative approach to achieving this challenge. It is because of this that the authors argue that it makes sense to consider an internal competitive edge, that of cultural competence.

Cultural Competence and Six Sigma

A way of explaining the importance of *culture* in cultural competence is best explained through means of the metaphor of Six Sigma. Organizations that have been successful in implementing Six Sigma, when asked, admit that the larger contributing ingredient of its success is more that of the cultural change, than the specifics of the system itself. When the late Bob Galvin, CEO of Motorola, first attempted implementation of Six Sigma back in the 1980s, it failed, as the major challenge faced by Motorola, while implementing Six Sigma, was the tendency of employees to fudge the system rather than make improvements (Tahiri, 2017).

> Robert William "Bob" Galvin was the son of the founder of Motorola, Paul Galvin, and served as the CEO of Motorola from 1959 to 1986. Motorola, Inc. was an American multinational telecommunications organization based in Schaumburg, Illinois, United States. After having lost $4.3 billion from 2007 to 2009, the organization split into two independent public companies, Motorola Mobility and Motorola Solutions on January 4, 2011. Motorola Solutions is generally considered to be the direct successor to Motorola, Inc., as the reorganization was structured with Motorola Mobility being spun off. Lenovo acquired Motorola Mobility in 2014.

Employees tried to improve the sigma level by increasing the number of opportunities for defects, like counting five opportunities for every solder joint, rather than by reducing defects. They also misunderstood that the improvement of a system should be aimed at what you want to achieve, not by what you do not want.

> 'A Six Sigma culture has the potential to literally transform employees. Those with Six Sigma certification are cultured to see themselves and the work they do differently than traditional employees. They are taught to: See work in terms of process flow, and not just departments and functions.'
>
> Villanova University

This was first explained, to our knowledge, in the work of the American physicist, Walter Shewhart. Shewhart married statistics, quality control, and process improvement in an era when quality control involved discarding defective items post-manufacture and is often regarded as the grandfather of total quality management and process improvement.

Walter Andrew Shewhart was an American physicist, engineer, and statistician, sometimes known as the father of statistical quality control and also related to the Shewhart cycle. He attended the University of Illinois at Urbana–Champaign before being awarded his doctorate in physics from the University of California, Berkeley in 1917.

Back to Motorola and Six Sigma though, Motorola eventually ensured the success of Six Sigma by making employees the stakeholders of the concept, when they realized that its successful implementation required a different approach, a different mindset, a different culture, and a different way of doing and being.

Motorola made it the responsibility of everyone to 'Define, Measure, Analyze, Identify, and Control the process improvement. This approach made workers understand that the purpose behind Six Sigma is an ingrained cultural change in the way of working. Six Sigma is not a system, it is a way of working.

The authors view and approach cultural competence in a similar manner, as an internal strength, a core competency, and a work culture. The motivation for redirecting competitive differentiation to an internal component that impacts the entire organization comes from the analysis across a broad spectrum of industry competitors. Furthermore, their ability to offer similarities, which is copied and imitated amongst rivals. Hence, the importance of finding a different way to compete.

Chapter Two: Key Takeaways

- Many organizations follow the taught models of exploiting the scale and scope of economies in pursuing sustainable competitiveness.
- Organizations do not necessarily view an internal strength when positioning themselves relative to competitors. Rather, they take an external view focusing on products and/or services, diversifying the application of their resources and taking advantage of imbalances in international labor practices and the associated costs.
- The effectiveness of performing a Porter's Five Forces analysis appears to rely more on the soft skills, than the hard skills component, for its

relevance, value, applicability, and contribution to organizational competitiveness. Therefore, organizations need to castle themselves by exercising cultural competence in dealing with the human systems of suppliers, buyers, government, and others, in such a way as to outperform competitors.

- Many organizations are successful at capturing and creating value, as these are mainly competitive attributes achieved through an external focus on product and/or service delivery. Delivering value however requires a deep-centered connection with customers, for which cultural competence is a key requirement.
- *Culture* in cultural competence is imperative for the successful application of cultural competence as it refers more to a way of being, than a system and/or process of implementation.

Castling

Cultural Competence as a Strategic Differentiator

Introduction

In Chapter One, the authors spoke more to the 'what' of cultural competence, and in Chapter Two, to the 'how' thereof. Chapter Three becomes practical as it begins to explain where to integrate cultural competence into the strategic planning process(es) of an organization. In doing so, the chapter brings the castling practice (cf. Chapter One and Two) to life. Castling, as previously stated, is the move in chess in which a player moves two pieces in the same move, and, once executed, it is almost impossible for the opponent to penetrate to the point of checkmate.

Cultural Competence within the Strategy Continuum

For the authors to explain where and how to integrate cultural competence into the strategic planning process of an organization, the authors use the strategy continuum in Lafley and Martin's, 'How Strategy Really Works.'

> How Strategy Really Works is a book about strategy, written by A.G. Lafley, former CEO of Procter & Gamble, and Roger Martin, dean of the Rotman School of Management. The book covers the transformation of P&G under Lafley and the approach to strategy that informed it.

In it, strategy is depicted as a coordinated and integrated set of five choices. With slight amendments to this continuum, the authors explain how cultural competence, as a thought paradigm, a dimension, and perspective, can be integrated into the strategic planning process.

The framework, depicted in Figure 3.1, illustrates the sequence of decisions taken in strategy formulation. The larger contextual and transactional environments within which the sequence of decisions is taken are

DOI: 10.4324/9781003303381-4

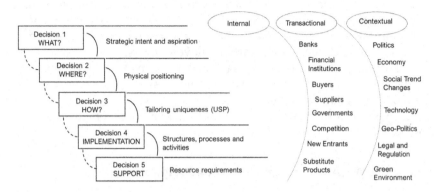

Figure 3.1 **Strategy Continuum Framework: Amended (Lafley & Martin, 2013). Illustration created by Marina van Zyl.**

added as amendments to the original motif of Lafley and Martin. The transactional environment refers to the environment that contains systems/institutions/people, commonly needed to enable a business to transact. Banks, financial institutions, buyers, suppliers, and governments are examples of such institutions. The transactional environment is also referred to as the market environment and/or the competitive environment. Porter's Five Forces Framework (cf. Chapter Two) consists of elements that constitute the transactional environment. Suffice to say that the transactional environment contains those human systems over which organizations have some or more levels of hierarchical influence.

The contextual environment, on the other hand, contains those spatial configurations like politics, economy, social trend changes, and technology. It is popularly known as 'PEST,' first published through Aguilar's research in 1967, referred to during the opening paragraphs of this book. (cf. pg. 3, 4)

Over time, components such as 'Legal' and 'Environment' was added and today, many organizations use the 'PESTLE' framework when scanning the business environment, and gathering data. A distinction between those components that make up the contextual environment, components over which organizations have little or no influence over, and those that make up the transactional environment, is necessary in understanding cultural competence as explained in the next paragraph.

Contextual components are spatial configurations, conceptualizations conjured up in the mind to help foster a better understanding of the larger business environment. Transactional components, or systems, are human systems. These are the systems organizations need to build a human relationship with; suppliers and buyers being examples. The hypothesis that the authors defend, is that a higher level of cultural competence will result in a stronger human relational bond with those factors of influence in the transactional environment, making the barrier to entry for competitors as impenetrable as the castling move in chess.

Referring to Figure 3.1, the transactional and contextual environments are depicted as the canvas upon which strategy, as a staggered number of decisions, are planned and executed.

Following is a step-by-step explanation thereof, incorporating cultural competence in each step.

Step One: WHAT (Strategic Intent and Aspiration)

In Figure 3.1, cultural competence is positioned as an influencer in each of the five steps which, together, constitutes the strategic planning process of Lafley and Martin.

In a way, this is an attempt at a tangible application of the idea of cultural competence being a drop of ink in a glass of water, which was explained conceptually in an earlier chapter of this book (cf. pg. 6, 11). Cultural competence refers to an approach and sensitivity as we embark on the discipline required in each of the five steps illustrated in Figure 3.1. As such, it represents a change in attitude, behavior, view, and perspective. As an example, the first step should consider cultural dimensions in terms of the intent of the strategy. In other words, the intent should not merely be to look at market wants and needs, shareholder value, and what the organization aims to achieve. It should do so, but with an enriched sensitivity of cultural dimensions and views in a participatory fashion when designing the intent in the first place.

The Airbnb Example

A practical example of castling through cultural competence is the Airbnb business model.

Airbnb, Inc. is an American organization that operates an online marketplace for lodging, primarily homestays for vacation rentals, and tourism activities. Based in San Francisco, California, the platform is accessible via website and mobile app. In December 2020, Airbnb was worth more than the three largest hotel chains globally after its trading debut. Airbnb's share price closed at $144.71, giving it a valuation of $86.5 billion. Marriott, Hilton, and Intercontinental were worth $84.1 billion combined at the time.

Airbnb's rise and success is based on the concept and practice of cultural competence, or at least, more than what people noticed, the authors argue. The question the authors aim to answer is why a rental model of accommodation became so successful when neither the host nor the renter knows one another? This question was the right question to ask as it addressed a seeming contradiction in how the business success of this scale normally works. The question is answered through reference to cultural competence as an influencer of the five steps in the strategy continuum displayed in Figure 3.1, Step 1 more specifically. A crucial factor that comes to mind is one of trust established through virtual contact. Trust itself requires physical proximity to aid the establishment of trust, as research suggests (Dhupia, Kumar, & Sahijwani, 2020). So, indeed only when customers trust a business, they regard it as credible and therefore are willing to do business with an organization. This means greater advocacy, loyalty, and engagement from customers.

Organizations tend to rely on reputational brand identity as the connector for customers to trust a product and/or service in the accommodation industry, as much as in most industries. Think of how you used to think about a trusted brand like The Hilton, versus how you first thought about Airbnb during the years of its inception. Yet, today, Airbnb is one of the largest, if not the largest, accommodation businesses in the world, without following the normal ownership model of owning their own properties that are for rent. With cultural competence as a critical component within the Airbnb business model, the authors noticed something different. There appears to be a progression and evolvement from traditional institutional trust (brand identity) to interpersonal trust between strangers, despite possible cultural differences. By focusing on cultural competence as a key differentiator and a core competency, Airbnb identified a human factor that enabled an exponentially faster and bigger growth for Airbnb than any of the well-known multinational hotel and accommodation businesses with which we are familiar. The authors' research points toward the notion that an enriched sensitivity of cultural dimensions and views, as well as a customer participatory design and construction element, enables identifying and leveraging trust. The mechanisms at play to further grow the business would therefore not just be the typical ones of labor, capital, entrepreneurship, market conditions, and so forth, which are the traditional components and remain important to understand, but also – and more importantly so – a culturally competent approach to the entire strategy continuum. This approach enables the identification of non-commercial components alongside or against commercial ones. The commercial ones typically being price points versus effectiveness, convenience, and affordability (cf. The introduction, page 2 when referencing a USP). The idea of positioning cultural competence as an influencer of thought, right at the start of the strategic thinking process – Step 1 of the continuum – is a possible way of ensuring cultural competence is considered in a structured manner, throughout the continuum.

Step Two: WHERE (Physical Positioning)

The same consideration is applied in executing the second step of the strategy continuum. For organizations, the geographic answer to where one could possibly compete, and should compete, has far-reaching implications on its overall strategic actions. Different geographical areas have different customer values, staff values, languages, beliefs, traditions, and behaviors. It is unwise to assume that what works in one region will do so in a blue-print fashion in another. One may argue that this is stating the obvious. Yet, many organizations still seem to struggle to differentiate between a culturally competent approach to different geographical regions, as opposed to a mere customization per market type and market segment.

Customization only refers to a modification according to a customer's individual preferences, whilst a culturally competent approach refers to a completely different engagement with a marketplace, namely a different business and operating model.

The impact of cultural competence in executing the second step of the strategy continuum is to enable organizations to progress from depending only on the marketing function for multinational customer engagement to infusing the entire organization with a new way of connecting with the diverse cultures of their customer base and staff mix. This is against the backdrop of different regional or country regulatory and other requirements.

The Netflix Example – How Not To Do It

This difference between customization and cultural competence, as a change factor in an organization's business model, was experienced by Netflix.

Netflix, Inc. is an American media services provider and production organization, headquartered in Los Gatos, California, founded in 1997 by Reed Hastings and Marc Randolph in Scotts Valley, California.

Today, many people know Netflix for its success in the live-streaming online entertainment business. It is the fascinating story of an unhappy customer, Reed Hastings (Founder and CEO of Netflix), who takes on the giant video rental chain, Blockbuster.

Blockbuster, officially Blockbuster LLC and formerly known as Blockbuster Video, was an American-based provider of home movie and video game rental services. Services were offered primarily at video rental shops, but later alternatives included DVD-by-mail, streaming, video on-demand, and cinema theater.

Blockbuster LLC was the largest American-based provider of home movie and video game rental services at the time of Netflix's creation. Hastings constructed a different business model through the effective use of technology and managed to deliver the same service as Blockbuster, but much more effectively, conveniently, and affordably. This resulted in Blockbuster going out of business several years later and Netflix soaring to a market capitalization of 165bn USD in 2018.

In 2019 however, the situation changed quite drastically against Netflix, which saw its share price tumble from almost 400 USD to around 285 USD. All in the space of about two weeks, and at the time of authoring this book, it was still struggling to pass 325 USD. A major contributing factor to this fall in share value has been attributed to the phenomenon of losing close to 125,000 subscribers in a noticeably short space of time and, for the first time, in its history. Reasons cited for this cancelation in subscriptions were, amongst others, increased competition, and poor content. However, a major reason, often overlooked by companies, especially those playing in the platform economy, was that of cultural preference. Cloud-based platform businesses often face this challenge. In the case of Netflix, certain content was considered to be distasteful and lacking sensitivity for different cultures, hence subscribers canceled the service in protest to this cultural incompetence.

The MTN Example – How To Do It

Providing a different example, one where the company 'got it right,' helps to further expand our understanding of the impact cultural competence can have when an organization embarks on expanding its global footprint.

An example is that of the mobile phone provider, MTN. More specifically, its Nigerian operations.

MTN Group Limited, formerly M-Cell, is a South African multinational mobile telecommunications company, operating in many African and Asian countries.

After the initial acquisition of the license to operate in Nigeria, Africa, MTN struggled to gain market share against that of previously well-established other operators in the market. Initially, it tried most of the well-known strategic approaches to market entry, the most popular one being that of price competitiveness. Still, it failed, until it discovered something unique, embedded in the culture of local Nigerians. This uniqueness is known by many as 'Ubuntu' and means, 'I am because we are.'

The word "Ubuntu" is from some southern African languages, and it literally means "humanness." To have ubuntu is to be a person who is living a genuinely human way of life, whereas to lack ubuntu is to be missing human excellence.

In Nigeria, ubuntu translated into a humanitarian behavior whereby family members would care for one another with a deep-rooted culture and tradition, enforcing this behavior. Parents for children, children for parents, brothers for sisters, and even, to further extensions of the family bloodline. So, based on this culturally competent insight, MTN started a campaign whereby family members got discounts on their phone calls when making calls to other family members, who also have a MTN contract. This transactional component was viewed and experienced as a tangible form of Ubuntu, should family members subscribe to the same service. The rest is history.

Reflecting on it today, it looks so simple but back in the 1990s it took a stroke of culturally competent genius to ignite the market share growth that followed. Today, MTN is one of the leading mobile phone networks across the African continent, following a similar model of cultural competence in the different countries it operates within.

To conclude, cultural competence allows for higher probability of success as organizations select to expand their offerings on a larger global scale. Be that through a traditional bricks-and-mortar model, or a digitized platform model. The principle remains the same.

Step Three: HOW (Tailoring Uniqueness – USP)

The third step in the strategy continuum considers an organization's competitive positioning and advantage. This is done through the selection of a competitive approach focusing on value-creation, value-capturing, or value-delivery (cf. Figure 2.3). The Master strategies that reflect either one or a combination of these competitive approaches are best described as low-cost or differentiation strategies. Both these Master strategy approaches have a significant focus on product and/or service delivery, which organizations communicate through a unique selling proposition (USP).

This is where cultural competence is distinctly different from the conventional differentiator approach models and the authors would like to draw specific attention to the following explaining this.

As mentioned in both Chapters 1 and 2, cultural competence should not be viewed as an external product and/or service differentiator. Even in the MTN example just explained, the differentiating strength and strategic competitive advantage lies internally with the organization's cultural competence. It is how culturally competent organizations think about their customers that gives them insight into offering a compelling offer. In the MTN case, this resulted in the Ubuntu-centric approach. Cultural competence speaks of a competitive differentiator and core competency as an internal driver of behavior within the organization. Thus, the impact of cultural competence, on the third step of the strategy continuum, refers to the ability of an organization to engage with a diverse customer base, and the complete transactional pipeline contained in Porter's Five Forces (upstream, in-, and downstream) in an authentic manner. Following on this, the business model is adapted to fit in with possible differentiated needs amongst diverse markets.

To understand this shift in thought paradigm better, the authors use the matrix in Figures 3.2 and 3.3 to elucidate further.

Displaying Figure 3.1 slightly differently, the authors elucidate Steps 2 and 3 as the positioning steps in strategy. Herein organizations decide on their scope of market penetration, as well as selecting the competitive advantage. Be that low cost or differentiation.

Although it might appear a bit academic and 'easy,' in a way, the positioning decision is not a default guarantee of sustained competitiveness. In

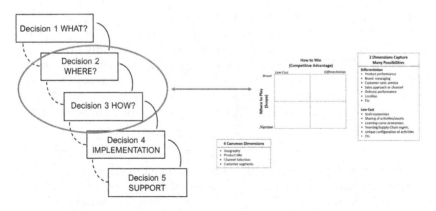

Figure 3.2 Strategy as a Positioning Act. Illustration created by Marina van Zyl.

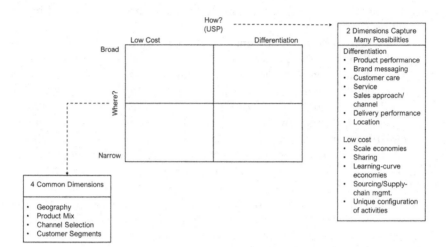

Figure 3.3 Strategic Positioning Dimensions (Lafley & Martin, 2013). Illustration created by Marina van Zyl.

many instances, it is more about creating a culturally competent decision-making process than the mere selection of a position in the market. And, as mentioned before, it stretches beyond the scope of customer as stakeholder to include up-, and downstream transactional components (Porter's Five Forces) as well.

Not being culturally competent about the external factors of influence can be as damaging as selecting the incorrect strategic position in the market.

The Woolworths Example – How Not To Do It

An example would be the South African retailer, Woolworths,' attempt to enter the Nigerian market in 2013. Although the organization applied steps two and three of the strategy continuum in strategically positioning itself in the Nigerian market, being differentiation and broad, the top right-hand quadrant of the matrix in Figure 3.3, it was the external factors of influence that led to this failed attempt. The authors do not include possible leadership bias, or even arrogance, in this example, but focus on the application of the strategy continuum steps, objectively.

Woolworths Holdings Limited is a South African multinational retail company that owns the South African retail chain Woolworths, and Australian retailers David Jones and Country Road Group. Woolworths, however, has no association with the UK and Australian Woolworths supermarket chains. These are low-cost, low-value groups in the UK and Australia, which are also called Woolworths. These are completely unrelated to the perceived high-value and high-quality product delivery model of Woolworths, South Africa.

In November 2013, Woolworths announced that its investment in Nigeria was no longer viable. In its own words, it cited high rental costs, import duties, and complex supply chain processes as the main reasons for failing. It is interesting to note that none of these reasons given were ones over which Woolworths had a high level of influence (cf. Contextual environment – systems over which organizations have little or no levels of hierarchical influence). However, the authors argue that it was not the low levels of influence that led to the failure of its operations in Nigeria. Rather it was Woolworth's lack of cultural competence toward these contextual factors of influence. In Nigeria, Woolworths displayed a lack of cultural competence related to the specific 'way of doing business' in the country.

Admitting that hindsight is perfect sight, we do need to consider the following display of lack of cultural competence. One of the factors that contributed to Woolworths' withdrawal from the Nigerian market was high rental rates and the non-negotiability thereof from the landlord's perspective. Although not officially recorded, companies that have expanded into Nigeria would know this. This is an example of a cultural difference between the industry in a region like South Africa versus that of Nigeria, in the case of retailers. Speaking of a kind of regional commercial 'way of doing business' as the cultural aspect referring to here, not the national or tribal culture as such. In South Africa, Woolworths was a well-established retailer and used to negotiate prime rental rates as an anchor tenant in shopping malls and other retail premises. This is a typical retail rental model, globally. In Nigeria, this rental behavior was not the case though, and it was therefore a requirement of Woolworths to adapt its business practices, and related model, to fit into the regional business operational culture. This adaptation and flexibility of mind requires an elevated level of cultural competence to understand this difference between two different regions of a similar industry, as well as an appropriate level of proper due diligence prior to entering the market, without ego and/or cultural bias.

Looking closely at organizations in a similar industry to that of Woolworths, it is interesting to note the distinct differences in business models of the successful versus the unsuccessful ones. Successful ones all have a common denominator – connecting with the local culture, both on a workforce/employment level as well as a customer level, and even more so on a supplier distribution and societal level. Considering Porter's Five (and a Half) Forces model, it may even include a governmental level. This is referred to at a later stage. Comparable retailers who 'got it right' in the Nigerian and other African country markets, would be companies like PEP Africa and the United Arab Emirates' Majid Al Futtaim, who acquired six stores operated by South African retail giant, Shoprite Holdings Ltd.

> **Pep Africa** has stores in five African countries. It is the biggest formal clothing retailer in Africa and has been providing families outside South Africa, its place of origin, with affordable clothing, footwear, homeware, and cellular products since 1995.
>
> **The Majid Al Futtaim Group** was founded by the late Emirati billionaire, Majid Al Futtaim. The company is a real estate and retail conglomerate, with projects in the Middle East, Asia, and Africa.
>
> **Shoprite Holdings Ltd** is Africa's largest supermarket retailer, operating more than 2,943 stores across Africa. The company's headquarters is in Brackenfell in the Western Cape province of South Africa.

Step Four: IMPLEMENTATION (Structures, Processes, and Activities)

To better explain the implementation of step four of the strategy continuum, the authors took a systemic view of an organization, referencing the work on organizational design of Dr. Elisabeth Dostal.

> Futurist, management consultant, and management educator, Dostal is the founder of Biomatrix Web, a management consulting organization that applies Biomatrix Systems Theory to management education and organizational and societal transformation.

According to Dostal, as a system, an organization consists of five internal inter-connected and inter-dependent aspects (Dostal, Cloete, & Jaros, 2005).

In the leadership realm, the two aspects most at play are that values, and strategic direction, illustrated in Figure 3.4, in the upper half of the center oval.

Whereas the purpose of values is primarily to anchor the behavior of the organization and its people, the purpose of the strategic direction is

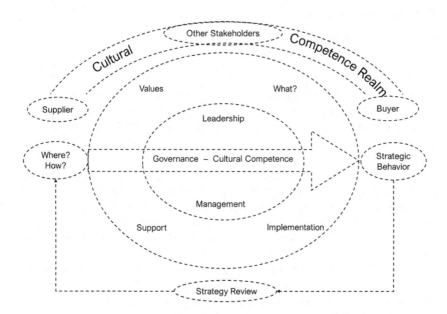

Figure 3.4 The Organization as a System. Illustration created by Marina van Zyl.

just that – to provide direction through its vision, mission, goals, and objectives. Referring to Figure 3.4, the original work of Dostal termed the organizational, vision, mission, goals, and objectives, by referring to it collectively as 'Aims.' Referring to the same figure, the reader will notice that the authors replaced this with the term 'What.' This change in terminology was made for easier alignment with, and referenced to, Step 1 of the strategy continuum. Like Dostal's term, it does, however, also include vision, mission, goals, and objectives of an organization.

In the management sphere of an organization, depicted in the lower part of the oval - in the same figure, there is a structure for implementation of the strategic intent, managed through systems. The authors amended Dostal's original drawing to align it with the amended strategy continuum framework and position 'implementation' (Step 4) and 'support' (Step 5) as such in the managerial realm.

Next, the authors draw Porter's Five Forces model into the systemic representation of an organization, to provide an additional dimension of managing the human component of the model, and for this, the authors refer to the physical logic of an organization. The physical logic stretches beyond the boundaries of the organization itself. It includes the physical positioning (proximity) of the organization in relation to its customers, suppliers, and other transactional factors of influence required to enable operations.

The Dell Example

In the authors' research, Dell Computer Company, came up as a good example to illustrate the meaning of physical logic.

> Dell is an American multinational technology company that develops, sells, repairs, and supports computers and related products and services, and is owned by its parent company of Dell Technologies.

Dell carries little inventory and therefore positions its suppliers in close proximity, physically. This suits the overall business model and allows for differentiation with customization and speed of delivery. It has well-established distribution supply chains, with specific Key Performance Indicators (KPIs) on delivery, irrespective of where they are situated, to integrate well with the internal physical logic of Dell's processes and activities. This aids its value proposition execution of offering affordable, customized computers, in record-breaking delivery time (cf. The introduction, page 2 when referencing a USP – effectiveness, affordability, convenience). See how the actual physical logic helps with the speed of delivery (close supplier proximity) and affordability (low inventory cost).

It is within the managerial sphere of the organization that policy choices are implemented, which determine the operational actions taken and behaviors displayed. Asset choices, related to the business model, include the use and application of tangible resources, and governance choices refer to how an organization cascades decision-making and levels of authority. To make it practical, operational actions might refer to managing shifts between full-time and part-time staff, whilst asset choices may relate to where factories are set up.

The first four aspects of viewing an organization as a system discussed so far, are:

- Values,
- Vision, mission, goals, and objectives (what – Step 1 of the strategy continuum),
- Implementation (Step 4 of the strategy continuum), and
- Support (Step 5 of the strategy continuum).

The fifth aspect is that of governance. Continuing the discussion in viewing the organization as a system, Governance, as the fifth internal aspect depicted in Figure 3.4, includes both the optimization of people performance as well as process alignment. Governance primarily drives implementation through people and, as such, it is here that internal cultural competence plays a pivotal role.

Note the arrow in the center of the system, in Figure 3.4, containing both the description of governance, as well as cultural competence, indicating the point of insertion. Linked to the fifth step of the strategy continuum, the people resource component plays a pivotal role in implementation, as mentioned previously. The late Jack Welsh is very well remembered for his quote: "Business success requires three things: people, implementation, and strategy – and in that order." (Welch, 2016) Working with people in a culturally competent manner ensures staff loyalty, customer satisfaction, and an overall higher probability of remaining holistically sustainable and competitive as an organization.

John Francis Welch Jr. – popularly known as "Jack" – was an American business executive, chemical engineer, and writer. He was Chairman and CEO of General Electric between 1981 and 2001.

Bearing this in mind it is further elaborated on in the fifth and final step in the adapted strategy continuum of Lafley and Martin.

Step Five: SUPPORT (Resource Requirements)

Staying with cultural competence, the fifth step in the strategy continuum includes people/human resources, financial, infrastructure, and information resources. Here, the authors focus on the people/human resource aspect.

The importance of cultural competence in this regard bears specific reference to the ability of selecting the right individuals and appointing them to the right positions within the organization, in the right geographical region. It needs to be an appropriate fit. The authors' research uncovered an alarming number of instances where the sustainability of organizations has come under threat due to a breakdown of people's relationships. These include internal and external relationships. Their research points to this breakdown being largely attributed to appointing the wrong people in the wrong positions and regions. A comparison of levels of success between the MTN and Woolworths example attests to this. The ability to attract, develop, and retain the right people in an organization reflects internal cultural competence with a strong positive correlation between cultural competence and the ability to apply people appropriately and accurately.

The BASF Example – How To Do It

A company that impressed the authors at the time of the research for this book, was BASF, the Germany-based European chemical company.

> BASF SE is a German multinational chemical company and the largest chemical producer in the world. Its headquarters is located in Ludwigshafen, Germany.

As the largest chemical producer in the world, the BASF Group comprises subsidiaries and joint ventures in more than 80 countries and operates 6 integrated production sites and 390 other production sites in Europe, Asia, Australia, the Americas, and Africa.

From their sustainability reporting, it is clear how the company focuses on cultural programs and training of its staff to ensure staff loyalty and engagement (sense of belonging), key components for establishing and growing internal cultural competence. It also applies cultural competence to increase customer loyalty and engagement and optimize diversity and inclusion. The inherent culturally competent attitude and behavior also inform their successful approach to regulatory matters, host governments, and business partners.

This example also integrates the components of culturally competent human relationships, as we have described it, being contained in Porter's Five (and a Half) Forces, across the spectrum of supplier, buyer, staff, and government. Through this example, it becomes clear that cultural competence needs to be applied across all the human relationship elements (cf. soft skills components of Porter's model) to be truly engrained in an organization's DNA. It does not help being culturally competent, for instance, when dealing with customers, but not applying the same to suppliers, internal staff, and/or government or other stakeholders in the business model.

Concluding Chapter Three, explanations, and examples of integrating cultural competence as a "drop of ink in" a glass of water by institutionalizing it in each of the strategy continuum's five steps were given.

Chapter Three: Key Takeaways

- Strategy is a sequence of decisions resulting in a differentiating competitive positioning for an organization relative to its competitors.
- The 'What' refers to the strategic intent and winning aspiration, the 'Where' to the market competitive positioning and scope/reach, the 'How' to the external unique selling proposition (USP), and resource

support refers to what is required for delivery and the implementation being the structures, processes, and activities of the organization.

- Cultural competence impacts significantly on each of the five decisions made in the strategy continuum and as such enables culturally competent organizations to shift from an external competitive advantage to an internal competitive advantage, effectively castling the organization's strategic advantage, making imitation, and copying thereof much more difficult for competitors. It creates an intrinsic unique strength.
- Business model design includes the physical logic of an organization and contains four components: resources, a unique selling proposition, profit model, and processes.
- Viewing the organization systemically, the governance aspect holds the key to setting the ground rules for successful culturally competent behaviors of influence across the entire transactional pipeline (Porter's Five Forces).

Chapter 4

The Satya Nadella Case for Cultural Competence

Introduction

This chapter provides an example from practice as adapted from the 'Satya Nadella at Microsoft: Instilling a growth mindset' case study by Ibarra, Rattan, and Johnston in June 2018.

Herminia Ibarra FBA is the Charles Handy Chair in Organizational Behavior, Professor of Organizational Behavior and Chair, Organizational Behavior Faculty at London Business School.

Aneeta Rattan is an Associate Professor of Organizational Behavior at London Business School.

The authors explain the application of cultural competence through the example of, at the time, Microsoft CEO, Satya Nadella and then move into addressing the question of how to measure culture competence.

Satya Narayana Nadella is an Indian American business executive. He is the executive chairperson and CEO of Microsoft, succeeding Steve Ballmer in 2014 as CEO and John W. Thompson in 2021 as chairman.

A recommendation of a three-dimensional measuring matrix, from here on onward refer to as a Cultural Competence Index (CCI), is put forward at the end of the chapter.

Nadella at Microsoft: Instilling a Growth Mindset

During an open interview with Goldman Sachs in December 2017, Nadella parts with the secrets of success in turning Microsoft around from

DOI: 10.4324/9781003303381-5

a company perceived as a Windows-centric lumbering elephant to a company valued at $700 billion, whose strategic bets on artificial intelligence and cloud computing were paying off. Nadella not only shares stories on this road to recovery during the interview, but he also talks about it in detail in his book, 'Hit Refresh: The Quest to Rediscover.'

He tells of how the organization, at the time of his being appointed as CEO, was plagued with internal employee animosity and, as he terms it, 'knife fights, bickering and inertia.' It was clear to Nadella that employee performance had become more important than customers and market opportunities. The culture of internal competition was stifling the once-leading tech powerhouse, and it was time for change – big change. Nadella realized he had to change the human system and set off doing just that through culture programs and training, which also resulted in changing Microsoft values. Of course, he did more than just that, but for purposes of highlighting cultural competence in practice, the authors focus on this specific initiative of Nadella.

Nadella followed in the steps of Steve Ballmer who had to lead the company through the post-2000 stock market crash and a decade during which a culture that crippled innovation flourished at Microsoft. During the interview with Goldman Sachs, Nadella refers to numerous failures in tech innovations they had to endure at the time, partly because of this toxic culture of internal competitiveness and lack of customer focus and customer centricity.

Nadella argued, at the time, that the culture was largely due to the systemic result of the performance appraisal and award system that, because of its forced distribution mechanisms, meant that one in ten people would always receive a poor rating, regardless of how much they contributed. In simple terms, the system focused on output, not on effort. As you can imagine, staff churn increased, internal sharing of ideas to foster innovation was not shared, and internal competition amongst staff members reached a fever pitch. Nadella recalls realizing how poorly this showed up on the sustainability reporting under staff loyalty and engagement, something needed to foster a climate of belonging. He chose to focus on the causal factors that led to this outcome to pull the scales right again. However, systemically there were other problems that also contributed to the culture at Microsoft that, although we do not focus on these as part of this book, are important to take cognizance of, as organizational leaders (Figure 4.1).

These were mainly external and referred to the reality that after the tech bubble burst and a plateauing stock price at Microsoft, people were not going to get wealthy. The kneejerk reaction to this was people turning on one another. Rather than contributing to the larger organization whereby, if the company succeeds, we all succeed, people adopted the behavior of

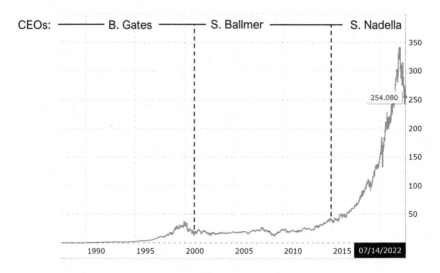

Figure 4.1 Evolution of Microsoft's Stock Price. Illustration created by Marina van Zyl.

each one for themselves, trampling on one another as the frantic climb to the top of the corporate ladder was the replacement methodology of achieving wealth, things being what they were.

Culture Programs and Training

Empathy, as one of the five key components of emotional intelligence (Goleman, 1995), is key to enabling cultural competence. During the interview, Nadella talks about their first child, Zain, who was premature, weighed just three pounds and had cerebral palsy. At the time of authoring this book, sadly, Zain had passed. At the time of his birth, Nadella recalled how he realized that empathy, 'was invisible and was a universal value and we had to learn that empathy is essential to deal with problems everywhere, whether at Microsoft or at home; globally.' Most important to note is that Nadella views empathy as a mindset, a culture, a way of living, and of being.

An engineer by qualification and clear systems thinking expert, Nadella actioned his attempt at changing the culture at Microsoft by pulling together some of the components that constituted sustainability reporting. In fact, he masterfully conducted all six components to form a beautiful musical, almost like an orchestra of sorts. He realized the necessity to change the culture through culture programs and training (components 1 and 2 of sustainability reporting). He started highlighting the importance of staff loyalty and specifically engagement in making Microsoft an industry leader again and did so by shifting the scope to customer loyalty and engagement (components 3 and 4 of sustainability reporting). He took the lead on managing and leading diversity better through inclusion and empathy, and in the final instance, enlarged Microsoft's social and environmental investment (components 5 and 6 of sustainability reporting). In the final instance, Nadella changed the performance management and reward system to create an environment in which cultural change could happen.

Transformational Leadership and Dual Transformation in the Context of Cultural Competence

One of the biggest challenges in immersing an organization in a macro change of this nature, especially improving the performance of cultural competence overall, is maintaining the momentum of the organizational operations and going ahead with business as usual. This difficulty stems from changing *the way* in which things are done, not necessarily *what* is done. It is also particularly difficult as the leadership characteristic to achieve the latter is more that of transformational leadership, than transactional leadership. The latter being more the style of Bill Gates himself, especially in the earlier days of Microsoft's creation and explosive growth.

Transactional leadership is more about compliance within an existing system and incremental change – a style more appropriate for a new organization going through explosive growth. Transformational leadership is more about changing a culture through radical change. Nadella was the first to admit that both Gates and Ballmer were very driven and super-smart, but also pacesetters in their leadership style. Their model was to question with precision, analyze ideas in meetings to test their validity and assess the presenter's conviction. What Nadella wanted though was a model encouraging curiosity, a hunger for learning, and empowering people to bring him new ideas and information.

Nadella managed to maintain a parallel implementation of these challenges, and the necessities of changing business as usual, by focusing on empowering employees and extending the external partnering agreements with previously deemed competitors. Most importantly, he created a culture of respect and influence in the organization, not of power and authority.

But Nadella did more than just harnessing cultural competence through programs and learning internally; he also extended this to the external stakeholders of the organization, primarily customers and business partners. This move enabled Microsoft to take the lead in some technical innovations again, whilst at the same time building cultural competence as an internal strength. He recalls how he drove customer visits and specific customer immersion initiatives whereby Microsoft employees would spend time with customers, in their world, to truly connect with their needs. These were initially met with resistance and seen as a waste of time and superfluous, but by persisting, it paid off. These actions were crucial as Nadella took employees from a *know-it-all* culture to *learn-it-all,* culture, a critically important component in engraining cultural competence (cf. Chapter One).

> Cultural competence is the successful application of cultural interests, awareness, understanding, sensitivity, and intelligence.

This behavior and actions from Nadella strongly support the point the authors made earlier (cf. pg.23, 24) regarding the true value of Porter's Five (and a Half) Forces. That the value of Porter's model lies more in the culturally competent dimension of the model, than in the attribute compilation of each of the different forces in the model (cf. Chapter Two, Fig. 2.1).

From 'Know-it-all' to 'Learn-it-all'

To change a culture is not easy – it never is - but for Nadella it was even more challenging. He followed in the footsteps of some of the most formidable leaders of the time, inherited a strongly ingrained culture, and, on top of this, had an extremely complex structure within which to bring about this change. Not only was it siloed in structure, but it was also competitive across departments.

Nadella refers to the Stanford psychologist, Carol Dweck, with a lot of respect as he talks about what he learned and implemented from her book, 'Mindset: The New Psychology of Success.'

> Carol Susan Dweck is an American psychologist. She is the Lewis and Virginia Eaton Professor of Psychology at Stanford University. Dweck is known for her work on motivation and mindset.

What Nadella got from the book is exactly what he needed to bring about the change in Microsoft. He needed to install exemplary cultural competence. From Dweck's thoughts and research, Nadella forged a plan for Microsoft. He deduced that Dweck divided the world between learners and non-learners. This was the clearest and simplest way he could demonstrate and understand the distinction between a fixed mindset, which will limit you, and a growth mindset, which can move you forward. Nadella concluded that Microsoft's culture change would center on 'the belief that everyone can grow and develop; potential is nurtured, not predetermined; and anyone can change their mindset.' He set out on this change mindset initiative and through culture programs and training gradually moved people from being 'know-it-all' to 'learn-it-all.'

Nadella continued by focusing on customer centricity externally, and diversity and inclusion internally, in order to achieve his organizational goal of achieving a 'One Microsoft.' He believed that Microsoft could be at its best if all employees actively seek and embrace diversity and inclusion. One of the most profound statements he made in this regard was that 'if we are going to serve the planet as our mission states, we need to reflect the planet.' From his book, 'Hit Refresh: The Quest to Rediscover Microsoft's Soul and Imagine a Better Future for Everyone,' Nadella argues that the diversity of Microsoft's workforce needs to continuously improve, and Microsoft needed to include a wide range of opinions and perspectives in their thinking and decision-making. Nadella used to appeal to people to make it possible for others to speak so that everyone's ideas come through. He drove inclusiveness which helped Microsoft become open to learning about their own biases and changing their behaviors so they can tap into the collective power of everyone in the company. He believed that it was through this culturally competent lens that their ideas, products, and customers would be better served.

At the time of authoring this book, the authors were of the view that there was no better example that proved the business case for cultural competence, than the actions of Nadella at Microsoft.

At this point, enough evidence to show the possible competitive advantage of cultural competence and the contribution it can make toward attaining a holistic competitive and sustainable advantage is displayed.

The question one now needs to ask is whether organizations can measure cultural competence and if so; can they improve it?

As it surfaced through the research, quantitative measurement of cultural competence is tricky, but despite this, many related diagnostics exist, such as those used in sustainability reporting. There is not yet a specific diagnostic measuring cultural competence in a quantitative manner for organizations. What the authors do have though, will now be explored.

Sustainability reporting has several variables. Some of these include:

- Culture (company or group)
- Leadership
- Stewardship
- Culture programs and training
- Staff loyalty, happiness, and engagement (sense of belonging)
- Customer loyalty and engagement

- Diversity and inclusion
- Staff programs with regards to social and environmental investment
- Relationships with governments and regulators
- Relationships with business partners
- Leading globally distributed staff and/or multicultural organizations

As can be observed by the nature of these variables, there are clear overlaps between this and what the authors advocate needs to be contained in an organization's ethos to qualify it as a culturally competent organization. However, not all organizations have sustainability reporting implemented as part of their governance reporting documentation. The design and use of a specific tool of measurement for an organization's cultural competence measurement is needed. In order to achieve this, the work of Kaplan and Norton, not using their Balanced Scorecard, but leveraging off the idea of a scorecard measurement to measure cultural competence, is investigated.

Robert Kaplan and David Norton are best known as the originators of the Balanced Scorecard, a strategic management tool that links a company's current actions with its long-term goals. The Balanced Scorecard is one of the most successful and widely used management tools in the world.

The cultural competence measurement tool is leveraged off existing assessments, generic in most organizations. Respective organizations may require some customization though and specificity in terms of what can be used in order to ascertain their cultural competence performance. Hence, a scorecard of sorts.

To ground the recommended scorecard or measuring matrix, the authors select to continue using the contextual framework provided when applying Porter's Five (and a Half) Forces, but with a focus on the culturally competent dimension (Chapter Two, Fig. 2.1), as well as other secondary sources related to cultural competence. These include Hofstede's entry modes concept, standard sustainability reporting, and various conceptual frameworks of management. Of these, the authors discussed the strategy continuum and depicted a view of an organization as a system. Deducting from these and other, Figure 4.2 portrays an initial picture of the CCI, as a measurement matrix.

The three-dimensional matrix variables selected for purposes of compiling a cultural competence measurement matrix are depicted in the motif presented in Figure 4.2.

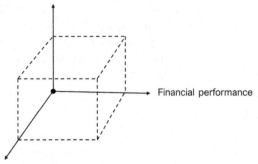

Z – External stakeholder loyalty

Financial performance

X – Internal/employee loyalty

Figure 4.2 Cultural Competence Index Measurement Matrix. Illustration created by Marina van Zyl.

The dimensions can be further broken down into examples displayed below:

- Internal/Employee Loyalty

  - staff engagement
  - staff turnover
  - average years at organization

- Financial performance

  - market capitalization
  - dividend declaration
  - sustainable profits
  - sustainable revenue

- External Stakeholders Loyalty

  - client/customer loyalty
  - business partners
  - government and government agencies

The above breakdown is an example of the suggested components for the matrix and may differ from one organization to another depending on their existing diagnostic and measurement tools. The detail on how to apply it is explained in the next chapter.

The breakthrough insight that the Nadella case study brings to the fore is the confirmation that national culture does not predict leadership behavior. Rather, it is the practice of open-mindedness for the purpose of learning from other cultures, which positions the leader as culturally competent and enables the possibility to establish it as an organizational competitive advantage. Furthermore, it is the ability to move beyond the mere transactional application of tools such as Porter's Five (and a Half) Forces, Hofstede's entry modes, sustainability reporting, and other forms of balanced scorecard measurements, to the relational application thereof, that creates the breeding ground for such internal competitiveness.

Chapter Four: Key Takeaways

- There appears to be a strong positive correlation between a growth mindset and the ability to adopt a culturally competent approach in relating to stakeholders in the up-, through-, and downstream components of an organization's transactional pipeline.
- A focus on people as opposed to focus on task performance can yield exponentially improved results; if it is driven through and guided by a culturally competent customer-centric approach.
- There are proven positive results from investing in people in an organization, provided it is done for the right reasons, is driven by top leadership, and has the development of people as a focus point, not just the increased performance of the organization.
- Cultural competence can be developed as an internal competitive differentiator for organizations and can be measured in a qualitative and quantitative manner for further improvement.
- Cultural competence has no correlation to national culture and can be embraced as a way of competing and a route to holistic sustainable competitiveness by any leader that is willing to regard cultural diversity as a primary source of learning.

The Cultural Competence Index (CCI) Measurement Matrix

Introduction

For cultural competence adoption into the DNA of an organization, the authors recommend a dual transformational approach which would allow for the continuation of the base-line business, ensuring continuity, whilst simultaneously bringing cultural competence into the realm of competitiveness. It would be necessary to consider this duality to explore ways of fusing business and cultural competence with one another, whilst avoiding too much business disruption. Realigning KPIs, as well as devising new ones, and redesigning organizational scorecard metrices, are but some of the structural components necessary to achieve positioning cultural competence as an internal competitive advantage. Chapter Five presents a measuring matrix to determine the Cultural Competence Index (CCI), and, as such, lay out the path to the mentioned transformation journey.

The pace of globalization and intensity of business environmental changes, all-be-it that there is also a growing pushback to globalization in some parts of the world, continue to challenge industries as competitive dynamics shift and new business models emerge. Given the challenges of remaining holistically competitive, the authors suggest companies critically review their current known business practices when it comes to what they know and, what they should do, to remain holistically competitive.

The research indicates that many organizations are struggling to develop an effective approach to transform the way they explore and exploit cultural diversity within their organizations, as well as diversity in their external relationships with customers, suppliers, and partners of sort. Business leaders tend to have diverse perspectives as to what cultural competence is and how to best optimize it. Some are pursuing cultural competence through activities of increased staff engagement, others through cross-cultural workshops when dealing with external stakeholders. Some are even investing in specific projects to bring about what they believe would be a

DOI: 10.4324/9781003303381-6

better understanding of diverse cultures. Cultural competence, however, is more than this, as explained in the preceding chapters. For real success to be achieved in improving an organization's CCI, the authors address the fundamental issue of underlying design logics of a culturally competent organization, as there appears to be a lack of conceptual clarity when it comes to cultural competence and how to reposition it as a strategic advantage. The authors aim to provide this clarity by first measuring cultural competence through the CCI, followed by the implementation of it, for improved performance of an organization as a whole.

With increased business competitiveness and complexity in having to lead multi-cultural global organizations, focusing on the human element in the transactional pipeline components (cf. Chapter One), there is a need for a more structured way in which to improve CCI performance. The secondary and primary resources consulted when authoring this book were not explicit about the pathway to implementing cultural competence, nor about how to measure it as an index, hence, the development of a measuring tool. Companies that the authors researched, like the Microsoft case study example discussed earlier (cf. Chapter Four), only showcase their successful outcomes of themselves when talking about how they leverage their ability to lead culturally diverse workforces to increase organizational performance. Examples of the structure of how to implement and how to measure cultural competence, however, are lacking from the research covered.

With this gap, the authors ventured on how to bring about the adaptation of various organizational functions, processes, and activities, in how they are being measured. This includes staff, customers, suppliers, and other stakeholders, plus the financial performance of the organization, hence, holistic competitiveness. All of these needs to be considered to achieve a step-change in the performance of the components of the transactional pipeline (up-, in-, and downstream). However, conceptually, the research yielded few examples of convergence on the underlying design logic of incorporating cultural competence into organizational competitiveness, from values, to strategy, to implementation. However, in guiding organizations in this transformation, the deficit is addressed through the proposal of a measurement matrix termed the Cultural Competence Index (CCI).

The chapter highlights the challenge of not having a basis to build on when presenting the matrix; yet builds upon prior research in seeking an in-depth understanding of the design logic underlying the performance of an organization's CCI. The authors looked beyond the pursuit of strategy as a primary building block of competitiveness, to understand how an organization needs to change fundamentally when embedding cultural competence into its model of competitiveness.

Questions addressed were:

- What are organizations seeking to become through this embeddedness of cultural competence?
- What is the underlying design logic of such organizations at the time of commencing with the pathway of this change?

In addressing these, and others, a new conceptual framework of measurement on the notion of a culturally competent organization was designed.

Positioning Cultural Competence

Referring to the required duality when wanting to transform whilst normal business operations continue, it is argued that organizations need to efficiently leverage existing resources and capabilities through known processes, and simultaneously combine resources and capabilities in new ways to result in new capabilities and further opportunities. The first being the current phases of strategy and implementation, measured against existing KPIs and a balanced scorecard of sort, whilst the latter implies embedding cultural competence into the competitive modeling of the organization. In responding to the challenge of how to lead a multicultural organization, it needs to be pointed out to there is a need of leveraging cultural diversity for enhanced performance. This can be done through active innovation and exploration of new opportunities, like experimenting with new holistic competitive business models, driven by the internal advantage of increased cultural competence. To balance the tension between the two pillars of dual transformation, a CCI measurement matrix, as well as a design logic for KPI alignment with existing scorecard categories, is suggested. This is done through reference to the variables of the CCI matrix, and the constructs contained in them and measured through a classification matrix. The latter is explained further in this chapter.

In a future where the human elements of an organization's transactional pipeline components are becoming increasingly culturally diverse, an increased CCI requires organizations to develop the capabilities to assimilate the mentioned transformation. The required shift in this transformation is from the traditional business-cultural diversity alignment perspective, where cultural diversity is dealt with on a functional level of Human Resources or Learning and Development, to cultural competence needing to be managed through formal structures, governance, and relational mechanisms as it is aligned to the business.

The transformation requires a renewed perspective of organizational strategy, as it drives competitiveness, whereby cultural competence is

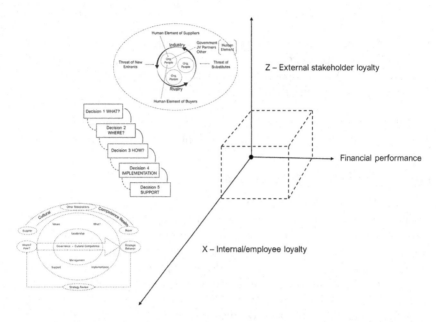

Figure 5.1 Complete Combined CCI Measurement Matrix. Illustration created by Marina van Zyl.

conceptually and structurally elevated to a position of a key success factor in achieving such increased competitiveness. Such an approach to cultural competence integration, when it comes to making it part of the strategy planning process, was discussed in Chapter Three. Building on this, the conceptual and structural positioning is graphically depicted in Figure 5.1. The graphical depiction of the CCI, which is necessary to understand how to apply the CCI measurement matrix, is explained in the components of the CCI Measurement Matrix.

Figure 5.1 contains three primary variables. These have been shown earlier in Figure 4.2. They are:

- Financial performance
- External stakeholder loyalty
- Internal/employee loyalty

Whereas the financial performance measurements follow globally standardized indices, the external- and internal-stakeholder variables are made up of constructs from three separate frameworks and are as such discussed in more detail below. The authors do not elaborate on the financial metrics as these are globally standardized indices.

The external- and internal stakeholder variables' constructs are derived from the following three separate frameworks:

- Porter's Five (and a half) Forces depicted in Figure 2.1 – more the relational (human – soft skills) aspects, however,
- The organization as a system, depicted in Figure 3.4 – more specifically the governance aspect of an organization, and
- The five steps in the amended strategy continuum framework, depicted in Figure 3.1.

The reader needs to bear the following in mind pertaining to sustainability reporting. There are overlaps between what the authors advocate need to be contained in an organization's system to qualify as a culturally competent organization, and the variables contained in standard sustainability and/or Environment, Social & Governance (ESG) reporting criteria. This being the case, sustainability criteria are not treated as separate individualized constructs in any of the three primary variables of the CCI.

Organizations can address these constructs and add them to the CCI measurement matrix if applicable. Thus, sustainability criteria are neither included, nor excluded, by the design of the CCI measurement matrix, but left to the applicability thereof per respective organizations.

To further provide clarity on the CCI measurement matrix, the authors extend the explanation by using three graphical depictions below. The reason for providing three graphical depictions is primarily to enhance the imagery, as a complete combined framework proves too difficult and impractical to present in print.

Figure 5.1 represents all the frameworks mentioned throughout the book containing elements contributing to the measurement of the two primary variables of the CCI measurement matrix, other than the financial dimension, being internal- and external stakeholder loyalty.

Each of the human-factor elements, allotted as constructs in the measurement matrix, discussed previously, are highlighted as to be the ones that need to be measured through a culturally competent lens.

The external stakeholder constructs selected from Porter's Five (and a Half) Forces are:

- Suppliers
- Government/JV Partners/Other
- Buyers

The internal stakeholder construct selected from Porter's Five (and a Half) Forces Framework, viewing the organization as a system, and the strategy continuum, combined, are:

- Internal people/staff, from Porter's Five (and a Half) Forces
- Governance, as one of the five internal aspects portrayed when viewing an organization as a system
- Support, as the fifth step in the amended strategy continuum framework

These are displayed graphically in Figures 5.2 and 5.3, with the selected constructs per framework, shaded in gray. Toward the end of the chapter, a consolidated version of the CCI measurement matrix is provided. To ensure the reader maintains a systemic view of cultural competence in an organization, all constructs are initially included in the measurement matrix drawings.

The external stakeholders' construct makeup is displayed in Figure 5.2. with the aid of the gray circles.

Next, the constructs applicable to the internal stakeholders' construct makeup is displayed in Figure 5.3.

Figure 5.3 presents an enhanced version of the internal stakeholder variable constructs selected from the afore-discussed frameworks and highlighted in gray. Referring to Figures 5.1, 5.2, and 5.3, the hypothesis the CCI measuring matrix is built upon is that a higher level of cultural competence, when managing the cultural competence constructs, will

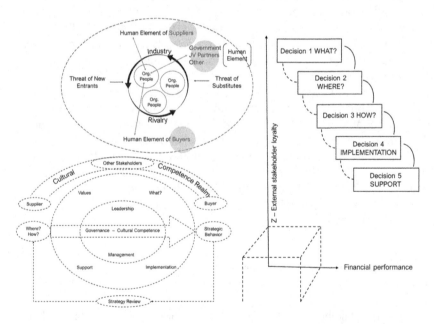

Figure 5.2 Constructs Applicable to External Stakeholder Loyalty. Illustration created by Marina van Zyl.

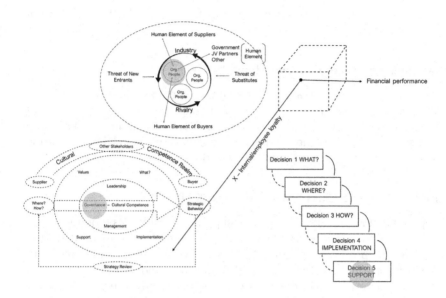

Figure 5.3 Constructs Applicable to Internal Stakeholder Loyalty. Illustration created by Marina van Zyl.

yield a higher probability of increased holistic sustainability, through an increased internal competitive advantage.

> *Note:* It is vital, at this point, to understand that the CCI measurement matrix does not measure the performance of each construct as a Key Performance Areas (KPAs), the way in which KPAs are measured normally. Rather, it focuses specifically on the cultural competence dimension of these constructs – termed as KPAs in organizational language – when analyzing the reason for the level of performance of each of them. In other words, a critical view is taken on the contribution of cultural competence to a performance level of a KPA.

To assist in understanding the complexities of the CCI measurement matrix, an example of one such a contribution of cultural competence in the performance of a specific KPA is provided. This is for illustrative purposes. Chapter Six elaborates further with case study examples on each of the CCI measurement matrix constructs. The example given here though is that of the external stakeholder loyalty construct, supplier.

As some of the indices mentioned are sensitive, where necessary, fictitious figures are used. Using the example, the accuracy of the indices figures is not important, but the principle of the application of cultural competence is.

Supplier Example: Woolworths in Nigeria

In Chapter Three, the authors referred to the unsuccessful attempt of Woolworths at entering the Nigerian market during the earlier part of this century. Using the same example here, an illustration is given of the structured inclusion of the cultural competence dimension when measuring KPAs. The explanation is hypothetical. It does however, prove the point.

Introducing the Classification Matrix (CM)

Suppliers, in Porter's model, include suppliers of all inputs required to run the operations of an organization. In this example, the focus is on the suppliers of property for rent, which gave Woolworths, at the time, premises to operate from. Having applied the same model they followed in other countries, Woolworths chose to rent, not to buy, the properties that would constitute their premises of operation. One can thus argue that their physical logic included rented property, and for successful management thereof, supplier management would need a way of ensuring flexibility and affordability on Woolworths' side. At the time of their closing down operations in Nigeria in 2013, Reuters reported that Woolworths cited this component as but one of the challenges they could not overcome.

> Reuters is a news agency owned by Thomson Reuters and is one of the largest news agencies in the world. The agency was established in London in 1851 by the German-born Paul Reuter.

Within the terminology of explaining cultural competence's impact on KPA performance, it is argued that the suppliers of premises, as a KPA, underperformed from Woolworths' perspective. It must be noted that, in this case, the underperformance was on how Woolworths managed the account and not on the Nigerian landlords per se.

The CCI Measurement Matrix and the Classification Matrix

To unpack the performance measured and recorded above, the CCI measurement matrix looks at whether addressing aspects of cultural competence can benefit KPA performance. The question is, how to measure the contribution/weight of cultural competence in a particular

KPA and whether it is quantifiable? To assist in this, the authors developed a Classification Matrix (CM). This provides a simplistic way of measuring the weight and/or contribution of cultural competence when analyzing the performance of a specific KPA. In order to understand this concept, an example of a specific CCI measurement matrix variable is looked at. In this case; 'external stakeholder loyalty.' The construct, which requires performance measurement – in this case, is Landlords. In the final instance, elements are identified that comprise the construct to be measured.

The CM Constructs and Elements

The construct makeup is the outcome of an iterative process of communication between the organization and a specific stakeholder – in this case, Woolworths, and the Landlord(s). The construct elements are not generic but specific to an organization and the position it finds itself in. So, hypothetically, had Woolworths researched the culturally competent constructs of supplier(s) in Nigeria's Landlord industry/culture, it is argued that it may have yielded at least some of the known elements when having to manage such a relationship in a similar scenario.

These would be:

• Local language proficiency
• Respect for people and the country
• Cultural understanding
• Negotiation ethos
• Professionalism
• Growth mindset
• Social acceptance

The list is not complete but makes a point that a culturally competent lens for this kind of analysis is a requirement, should the organization want to leverage cultural competence as a way of increasing KPA performance. It is specific though and argues that organizations need to determine which cultural competence construct elements should be included, for them, when measuring the specific CCI variable and related KPA. Once agreed upon, the performance of these constructs can be measured, through its element makeup, by those on the receiving end of the organization's KPA being measured. If the KPA is supplier performance, the supplier(s) need to do the rating. Completing the CM, the supplier(s) also need to indicate how important the identified construct elements are relative to one another.

Figure 5.4 further clarifies how the contribution of cultural competence to KPA performance is measured.

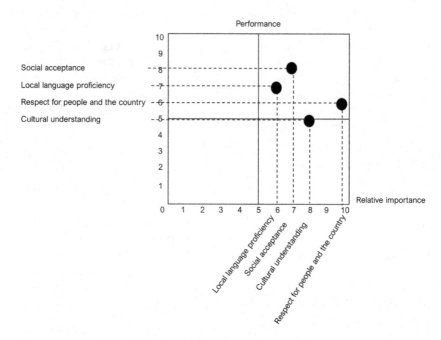

Figure 5.4 Classification Matrix – Supplier/Landlord. Illustration created by Marina van Zyl.

The CM in Practice

A CM consists of a 2-by-2 matrix made up of two independent variables. Unlike most 2-by-2 matrixes, both variables are independent. The measurement is done in a reflective manner, asking the receiver of the aspired culturally competent behavior, to rate the performance thereof, and how important the specific variable elements are relative to each other. Figure 5.4 is a graphical display of the CM. Four of the seven elements in the Woolworths hypothetical example are selected for display purposes. Along with the CM displayed in Figure 5.4, Table 5.1 contains more information pertaining to each of the identified variable elements. In the CM, the X-axis represents a relative score of the variable elements measured and how important they are relative to one another. In the example, it must be noted that local language proficiency, for example, is less important to the supplier, as a culturally competent variable element, than that of cultural understanding, for example.

In the CM, the Y-axis represents the performance on a scale of ten for each measured variable element. An agreed-upon definitive description of the variable elements is provided in a table format, in Table 5.1, along with the measured performance and relative importance ratings. The

Table 5.1 Results of CM on Supplier Performance Cultural Competence Dimension

Elements	Agreed description	Performance	Relative importance
Local language proficiency	Basic greeting and curtesy jargon to be mastered	7	6
Respect for people and the country	Display a genuine willingness to learn from the people of the host country	6	10
Cultural understanding	Understand why business is conducted in a locally unique way	5	8
Negotiation ethos	Adapt to the negotiation practices of the host country	5	9
Professionalism	Treat potential business partners as equals	7	9
Growth mindset	Display a willingness to be flexible in current business model	4	10
Social acceptance	Blend with the social practices of the host country	8	7
Rounded average		6 (60%)	

agreed definition referred to here is based on the agreement between the organization and those who rate the performance. In this example's case, Woolworths as the organization, and the Landlord as the one(s) to give feedback via a rating scale.

The rounded average, as a total, indicates the level of cultural competence performance achieved by the organization as rated by the receiver of such performance, in this case, the cultural competent performance of the construct, Landlords.

In simple terms, as illustrated in Figure 5.2, the CCI component of external stakeholder loyalty consists of:

- Suppliers
- Government/JV Partners/Other
- Buyers

The supplier construct measured in this hypothetical case is the Landlord (s). The cultural competence elements that is used to measure performance with, are:

- Local language proficiency
- Respect for people and the country
- Cultural understanding

- Negotiation ethos
- Professionalism
- Growth mindset
- Social acceptance

The overall performance for this specific construct's cultural competence is 60%. This percentage does not reflect the measurement of the KPA. It reflects the performance of cultural competence displayed in engaging with the Landlord(s) as part of the larger more comprehensive supplier management KPA.

Interpreting the Cultural Competence Contribution in a KPA

The question is, what does the overall performance percentage mean? In the Woolworths hypothetical example, possible reasons for the perform-ance of the 60% might be that the organization is not very competent in the understanding of the cultural understanding and growth mindset ele-ments of the Landlord(s) construct. The organization tends to display a lack of understanding of how important cultural understanding is to the Landlord(s), when dealing with international organizations, not native to Nigeria. The same can be said of their expectation that these companies need to have a growth mindset and try to have a better understanding of the industry culture, or way of doing business, through learning more about it. For this, an open mindset, or growth mindset, is required.

A further interpretation of the "fictitious" results in this example can be that it would appear that the organization being measured does not show a genuine respect towards people in the host country. Their cultural under-standing is low, spilling over into an equally poorly performing negation ethos.

The next steps for the organization would be to reflect on each of the construct elements' ratings and to improve the element measured.

Full Application of the CCI Measurement Matrix

This method of measurement needs to be repeated for all three variables of the CCI measurement matrix, identifying the relevant constructs that make up the variables, and their respective elements. Construct elements iden-tified for the CM will differ from organization to organization. In the final instance, it is important to bear in mind that the CCI measurement matrix focuses on the contribution that cultural competence makes toward overall KPA performance. The aim is *not* to deduct direct correlations in terms of high- or poor performance. The aim is to investigate the possibility that a higher CCI can positively impact overall organizational performance, enforcing cultural competence as an internal competitive advantage and contributor to holistic sustained competitiveness.

This concludes the explanation of the application of the CCI measurement matrix relating to a specific KPA. In Chapter Six, a case study is done of the other variable constructs and their elements in a summative descriptive format.

CCI Simplified

A simpler version of the motif representing the CCI as to the one portrayed in Figure 5.1. is displayed in Figure 5.5. This motif represents the constructs of financial performance, internal stakeholder loyalty, and external stakeholder loyalty CCI variables. The motif depicts these variables as circles, with the juncture in the center, representing the overall CCI measurement.

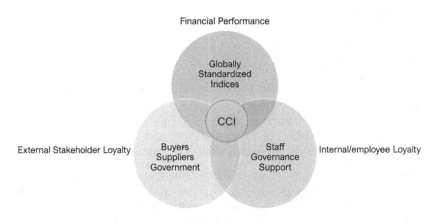

Figure 5.5 CCI Simplified. Illustration created by Marina van Zyl.

Chapter Five: Key Takeaways

- For cultural competence adoption into the DNA of an organization, a dual transformational approach is recommended. This would allow for the continuation of the baseline business, ensuring continuity, whilst simultaneously bringing cultural competence into the realm of competitiveness.

- With increased business competitiveness and complexity in having to lead multicultural global organizations, focusing on the human element in the transactional pipeline components, there is a need for a more structured way in which to improve the CCI performance.
- For purposes of designing the CCI measurement matrix, there are three variables
  - Financial performance
  - Internal stakeholder loyalty
  - External stakeholder loyalty
- Internal stakeholder loyalty has three constructs
  - Staff
  - Governance
  - Support
- External stakeholder loyalty has three constructs
  - Buyer
  - Supplier
  - Government/other stakeholders
- The internal and external stakeholder loyalty constructs are extracted from three separate frameworks
  - Porter's Five (and a half) Forces depicted in Figure 2.1 – more the relational aspects, however,
  - The organization as a system, depicted in Figure 3.4 – more specifically the governance aspect of an organization, and
  - The five steps in the amended strategy continuum framework.
- In the final instance, to achieve cultural competence through KPA focus, organizations need to identify the most important human elements with respect to selected KPAs. Then, take each KPA and apply a classification matrix that applies human elements to that KPA and identify the relative importance and performance of the organization against each such human element.

Case Study Example Explanations of the CCI Construct Elements

Introduction

Continuing with the example explanations of the various CCI construct elements, Chapter Six provides case study examples of buyers, government/other stakeholders, staff, governance, support, and financial performance.

Buyer Example

The Woolworths/Nigerian example is studied. Reuters also reported that Woolworths pulled the plug on its Nigerian business citing the difficulties of marketing to consumers in Africa's most populous country. Analysts were of the opinion, at the time, that the more basic issue was marketing to wealthy mobile and brand-conscious Nigerians, and Woolworths was not yet a big brand in Nigeria.

A higher level of cultural competence would have revealed that wealthy Nigerians that fell in their target market segment, tend to fly to London and bring items back in suitcases, or would prefer to spend money on traditional tailor-made clothes or an expensive fashion label. A combination of an inside-out as opposed to an outside-in approach (cf. Figure 2.2) to the market, coupled with a lack of cultural competence to heighten customer engagement, led to Woolworths being ignorant of this fact, for one, and led to their failure in Nigeria. A number of big brands were investing in Nigeria at the same time, like Burberry, and Tommy Hilfiger. These up- or mid-market brands were well-known by Nigerians. They read the market's 'wants and needs' effectively by understanding their customers better. The latter again being a function of cultural competence.

As with the supplier/landlord example explained in the previous chapter, a CM measurement of the construct elements applicable in this scenario, could have led to similar insight, had the company adopted a growth mindset as a prerequisite to enhancing its own cultural competence toward the market.

DOI: 10.4324/9781003303381-7

Experts might argue this point and say that this is purely market intelligence related and not necessarily a function of cultural competence. If that is the argument, then cultural competence is not understood in its application. Chapter One gives a clear distinction between cultural interest, -awareness, -understanding, -intelligence, and -competence. Cultural interest refers to people relating to specific aspects of cultures other than their own and Cultural awareness, on the other hand, is primarily associated with a level of understanding of the differences between nationalities and cultures. Cultural understanding is elevating awareness of culture to an attempt of comprehending it, specifically for the purposes of building cross-cultural relationships and optimizing the strength in that. Cultural knowledge and understanding helps one in shaping a unique perspective on matters, framed through the cultural lens of someone else's different, culturally informed, view. In a way, this relates to cultural sensitivity. Cultural intelligence is considered when entering into another (host) country.

All of these descriptors of cultural diversity can be defined through market intelligence, but that still does not mean an organization would redesign its business model in response to that. Woolworths/Nigeria being a case in point. Only cultural competence can spur an organization to act through a growth mindset, based on the knowledge gained from market intelligence.

The third construct in the explanation of the CCI measurement index variable of external stakeholder loyalty follows.

Government/Other Stakeholders Example

The importance of cultural competence toward the government of a host country is further explained with reference to the Chinese Government – in this particular example. However, it needs to be noted that the same principles may be relevant to examples of other partner stakeholders. It is about the principle and not the content of the example being cited.

In this particular example, cultural competence refers to the contextual intelligence of a particular government and how, being uninformed or ignorant of the ethos of a government, can lead to a higher risk in the chosen business model.

An example is the case study of the a2 Milk Company (A2MC) (Esty & Fisher, 2019).

The a2 Milk Company Limited is a dual-listed NZX and ASX 50 public listed company that commercializes intellectual property relating to A1 protein-free milk that is sold under the a2 Milk brand and related products such as infant formula.

There have been numerous case studies on the strategic wisdom of this company, cited by numerous Business Schools for more than a decade. For the purpose of explaining the cultural competence component relevant when dealing with a government, as one of the variable constructs of the CCI, the focus is on specific sections of referenced case studies, being the regulation of the milk industry. The regulation relevant in this case is that of regulation inspired by national interests, as well as ethnic specificity, such as the Chinese government's regulation of child-birth numbers.

The cultural competence construct at play in this example offers a fascinating look at a unique dimension of cultural competence. This becomes possible as cultural competence is incorporated as a filter or lens as alluded to in Chapter Three – when integrating cultural competence into the five phases of the strategy continuum. In this example, cultural competence can help organizations to ascertain and proactively hedge themselves against possible increased risk and exposure, should nationalist-inspired regulations and pressure on a lower birth-rate 'allowance,' be implemented by the government.

A backdrop for this is that in on 23 February 2017, two days after the a2MC announced a new strategic relationship with Fonterra Co-Cooperative Group, the a2MC became the most valuable company on the New Zealand Stock Exchange. In just over a year, its market value rocketed from NZ$2 to NZ$10 billion.

Fonterra Co-operative Group Limited is a New Zealand multi-national publicly traded dairy co-operative owned by around 9,000 New Zealand farmers. The company is responsible for approximately 30% of the world's dairy exports and is the largest of its kind in New Zealand.

At the time, the company produced drinking milk and infant formula, primarily in China and Australia. The a2MC differed from other dairy processing companies as it sold products containing the A2 beta-casein protein. This genetic test, developed by the a2MC determined whether a cow produced A2 or A1 type protein in its milk. Most cows produce A1 protein. Eliminating the A1 protein from dairy products was significant because many people have difficulty digesting A1 milk. A2 milk has several health benefits and is easier for people with milk intolerance to digest.

Despite the success of the company on the open market, it had an interesting relationship with the Chinese government, as the latter had imposed a regulation throughout the period that the a2MC invested in the

Chinese market; sometimes favoring the company; sometimes not. An example was the government-imposed pricing control of 2013 that disadvantaged the a2MC share price; understandably so. The reason for the drop in share price, at the time, was that the pricing control severely exposed the a2MC as a2 Milk's China label business – which represented 45%, at the time, of its infant formula revenue – operated in the ultra-premium sector.

Besides these regulatory disruptions, there have been times throughout the period of the a2MC's expansion into the Chinese market, where Chinese consumers would prefer and have increased favoritism toward domestic brands.

Cultural competence is at play here. The question is posed of how it is measured. It must be understood in the realm of understanding a government. A closer look at this example of price control, in 2013, is that it is an organization's CCI, specifically the government construct, which will enable better judgment of whether a government, in this case, the Chinese government, might go as far as implementing impacting regulations of sort. The cultural competence dimension, being the Chinese government's style of controlling markets and the motives driving it, which might be nationalist and human by nature.

From the referenced case study, it is interesting to note that the Chinese government favored domestic infant formula brands and after 2019, it had set targets for local players, in the market, to make up 60% of consumption within three years. Integrating culturally competent elements into a scenario related to risk, one can argue that the a2MC could have been prompted to have considered nationalist drivers that could contribute to possible price control regulation. An example of this could be an increase in China's birth rate and how this might prompt the Chinese government in either direction related to price controls and possible localized distribution quotas, determined by the government, or not. The culturally competent aspect at play in such a scenario is for the a2MC to know that increases in birthrate will likely occur in regions relying on locally made formula brands due to price sensitivity and affordability.

The CCI is a weighted index, illustrated in Figure 5.4 and Table 5.1. There are three variables; Financial Performance; External-, and Internal Stakeholder Loyalty. This is displayed in Figure 5.5. The a2MC case study illustrates how, even though the CCI consists of three variables, each with its own constructs, it should not be applied in a siloed manner, which is when a company has groups of experts separated by department, specialization, or location. A siloed approach leads to organizational department goals being pursued, instead of holistic organizational goals, impacting negatively on sustained holistic competitiveness. In the case of the a2MC, this siloed approach led to the underplaying of inventory (reference) and impacted negatively on the holistic performance of the organization. Focusing on one variable of the CCI, in this case, the financial performance variable, skews the attempt of balancing the triangulation between all three variables of the CCI.

To prove this point, the a2MC has been exemplary in how it applied its cultural competence when dealing with the Chinese government, as well as the traditionalist Chinese consumer. The financial metrics, however, of inventory holding were hugely underplayed and led to a fall from grace for the a2MC during 2021, following a period of low sales, hugely impacted on by the COVID-19 pandemic and resulting international government-imposed lockdowns. The incredible growth the company experienced and its steep fall from grace in 2021 split the market over its prospects for recovery. It was predicted that the first half of 2022 sales would be down for the English and Chinese label formula. This was due to the a2MC deliberately constraining products to deal with its aging inventory issues, a factor of poor inventory management. This led to mixed signals for the a2MC's pricing and the age of their in-market inventory. This is important since Chinese mothers view formula over 12 months old as aged and spurn it. The latter being a cultural competence factor of influence. The lack of insight into this factor, blended into financial metrics not well managed, tumbled the a2MC's sustained holistic competitiveness.

The case study proves the importance and validity of cultural competence and the need of incorporating the financial performance variable into the CCI measurement. All three CCI variables need to be constantly kept in check, otherwise, one construct of one variable can influence the result considerably negatively.

This concludes the external stakeholder variable case study examples of supplier(s), buyer(s), and government/other partners. The example also included a financial metrics dimension to be considered, and how to do this. A discussion follows about the internal stakeholder variable case study examples of staff, governance, and support.

Staff Example

As numerous external and independent organizations have recognized the Boston Consulting Group (BCG) for their impeccable rating on the staff component of their sustainability reports, it is an appropriate example to illustrate how to effectively apply cultural competence to the staff construct of the internal stakeholder loyalty variable of the CCI.

The following are studied:

- International Opportunities
- Career Development

- Training and Development
- Apprenticeship
- Educational Support
- Secondment
- Career Sustainability

These construct elements are common to most sustainability reports, however, not all organizations have sustainability reporting as part of their governance structures implemented already. Therefore, the authors recommend that these can be used as the construct elements when constructing a CM, described earlier in Chapter Five. Organizations can also, amend these to fit the uniqueness of their own organization.

As alluded to the supplier, buyer, and government/other constructs of the external stakeholder loyalty variable of the CCI thus far, with the supplier being the example illustrated, a repeat application is to be presented, citing the staff constructs. The construct elements chosen for the CM in this example, are those mentioned as per BCG's sustainability reporting criteria. Details of the agreed-upon definitive description of the culturally competent construct elements are provided in a table format, in Table 6.1, along with the measured performance and relative importance ratings. The latter two are provided as a hypothetical scenario for purposes of explanation. In mining further into cultural competence implementation at BCG, it became apparent that BCG drives staff loyalty and engagement as one of the pillars of embedding cultural competence throughout the organization. This is done in order for the staff to be in a position to experience a sense of belonging, which requires high dosages of cultural competence. Referring to the sustainability report (2018), staff at BCG bears witness to the fact that working at BCG means support, inspiration, flexibility, and countless opportunities to grow and learn. The financial sustainability motivation, however, is that as the business grows, staff opportunities increase, which is a motivation for staff members. Based on the same analysis and interpretation as illustrated in the supplier example in Chapter Five, "career development" in this hypothesized BCG table, needs further analysis in search of possible deficits of cultural competence.

Taking all into account, it is recommended that organizations who do not have existing sustainability reporting items can use top-performing companies, such as illustrated in case studies in this book and use their elements as a starting point to construct their own.

Table 6.1 Results of CM on Staff Performance Cultural Competence Dimension

Variable	Agreed description	Performance	Relative importance
International Opportunities	Encourage our staff to become global ambassadors.	8	6
Career Development	Offers continuous feedback, semiannual reviews, and an individually assigned career development advisor who helps staff craft and execute a development plan.	6	10
Training and Development	Receive up to four and a half weeks of training and development in the first year, and at least one week every year thereafter.	7	8
Apprenticeship	Offer day-to-day guidance and support from the project leader on a staff member's case, fellow teammates, and a mentor.	7	9
Educational Support	Provides financial support for professional education and advanced degrees.	9	9
Secondment	Work for up to a year in a secondment position for private sector clients around the world or for global partners in social change.	8	10
Career Sustainability	All employees have access to programs that provide eligible staff with flexible work options, such as part-time arrangements or the opportunity to take an extended period of time off.	9	7
Rounded average		8 (80%)	

Governance Explanation

A number of critical factors relating to this construct are explained below, looking at why governance is important for the institutionalization of cultural competence, and how to embed cultural competence within an organization's advisory bodies, policies, standards, and goals.

It was established that cultural competence requires an organization-wide approach to the pillars of management to succeed in its impact on holistic sustainable competitiveness. This includes planning, implementing, evaluating, and controlling, and value-added by supporting internal and external stakeholders' of culturally diverse backgrounds. Meaningful culturally competent strategies need to be embedded in the core business of the organization, and filtered through to the core support, and organizational support processes, ensuring that 'drop of ink in a glass of water' effect. Policies and systems need to guide the actions of the boards, executive leadership, management, and staff implementing the thinking, to ensure consistent regulated cultural competence implementation and application in behavior.

Referring to Figure 3.4, governance, although a variable construct of the CCI in its own right, has a strong systemic relation with the other constructs in ensuring the institutionalization of cultural competence. Policy, with a cultural competence dimension, is required for all the constructs, being supplier, buyer, government/other, staff, and support. The latter being the last of the constructs of the internal stakeholder loyalty variable of the CCI to be discussed.

Support Explanation

Referring to the prior discussion on the strategy continuum, the fifth step, support, (cf. Figure 3.1) includes the four generic resources all companies are dealt with. These are human resources, financial-, infrastructure-, and information resources. Cultural competence focuses on human resources as a construct of the internal stakeholder loyalty variable of the CCI. In the case of support, as a construct, the importance of cultural competence bears specific reference to the ability to select the right individuals and appoint them to the right positions within the organization, in the right geographical region. With reference made to this point see Chapter Three.

The third variable of the CCI, financial reporting, is discussed next.

Financial Reporting Explanation

When it comes to the CCI, the authors recommend including typical financial performance measurements in measuring the financial performance variable. These include Gross Profit Margin, Net Profit Margin, Working Capital, Current Ratio, Quick Ratio, Leverage, Debt-to-Equity Ratio, Inventory Turnover, Total Asset Turnover, Return on Equity, Return on Assets, and Operating Cash Flow.

The a2MC case study illustrates the systemic nature of financial reporting when measuring cultural competence. Suffice to mention that it is agreed that the cultural competence dimension in all of the mentioned constructs of supplier, buyer, government/other, staff, governance, and support, is imperative. However, focusing on this in such a way that it leads to a possible detrimental impact on the financial performance of an organization, defeats the purpose of the exercise and creation of holistic sustainable competitiveness. The aim of the CCI is to determine the role of cultural competence in "lifting" it and maintaining holistic competitive sustainability with financial performance being key in the equation.

The Inclusion of Sustainability Reporting

The importance of variable constructs elements of the CM remains specific to each organization. Therefore, where applicable, sustainability reporting components can be considered to be included when organizations compile/develop their CCI variable construct elements.

Chapter Six: Key Takeaways

- Cultural competence can spur an organization to act through a growth mindset, based on the knowledge gained from market intelligence.
- Financial performance can be improved through higher levels of cultural competence.
- A systemic approach is required in managing and measuring the independent constructs of each of the three variables of the CCI, determining interdependencies, foreseeing, and understanding the impact of one on the other(s).
- Existing sustainability reporting criteria of an organization can be a starting point for organizations in designing cultural competence measurement through a CM from scratch.
- Financial performance is part of the balance in the triangulation between it and internal and external stakeholder loyalty variables, completing the CCI.

Institutionalizing Cultural Competence

Introduction

It is common that organizational structures are in place within organizations and utilized as the canvas for operational activity implementation. This holds true for any organization. It, however, was established that in several cases, the business parts of strategy, vision, mission, goals and objectives, and competitive models, are often managed separately from an institutionalized cultural competence embeddedness. Although cultural competence refers to the manner of work and behavior, it is often not in a standard Balanced Scorecard measurement, or other similar tools and/or frameworks of organizational sustainability, competitiveness, and performance. It could be partially reflected in sustainability reporting, by some organizations, but this practice is not performed by all companies. Thus, a separate focus is required to ensure the institutionalization of cultural competence in all organizational activity systems; Core-, Core Support-, as well as Organizational Support activity systems, also referred to as processes.

The institutionalizing of cultural competence should start with reevaluating how organizations are designed structurally (cf. Chapter Five – design logic). This should be done with a view to redesigning the way organizations guide behavior in performing its functions, work, and operations. The focus should be to shift the focus from resource allocation to the outcomes measured through the CCI measurement matrix. Organizations can easily embark on practicing cultural competence as an alternative to conventional models of competitiveness.

Organizations intending to successfully institutionalize cultural competence boundaries should be extended beyond the practice thus far in driving a mindset shift from merely considering cultural competence in a behavioral sense, to being culturally competent to the core. This can be done through the redesigning of an activity system (see next paragraph), coupled with a cultural change initiative, following existing well-known change process frameworks.

DOI: 10.4324/9781003303381-8

Activity System Redesign

Reference to business model flexibility is embarked upon. Post that, exploring of frameworks assisting with the cultural change needed to shift the organization from cultural competence in a behavioral sense, to being culturally competent to the core. The following business model of Figure 7.1 is a reference.

To contextualize the impact of cultural competence institutionalization, an adaptation of Clay Christensen's business model is referred to.

> Clayton Magleby Christensen (also popularly known as 'Clay') was a Harvard Business School Professor who developed the theory of "disruptive innovation", which has been called the most influential business idea of the early 21st century.

Figure 7.1 depicts four key components of a business model. The top left in the motif is the value proposition, previously referred to (cf. pg. 33) as the USP (Unique Selling Proposition). This is co-contributed by the variables of effectiveness, affordability, and convenience (cf. Dell example – Chapter Three).

Top right of the motif are the resources mentioned prior; human-, financial-, information-, and infrastructure. These are generic to all organizations and, although they can differ in quantity and quality, remain

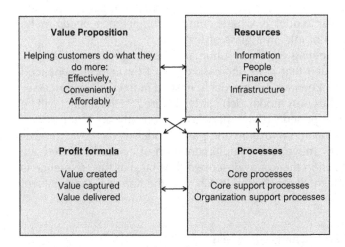

Figure 7.1 Business Model: Amended (Johnson, Christensen, & Kagermann, 2008). Illustration created by Marina van Zyl.

constrained to only these four. Organizations do not differ in resources; they differ in the application thereof. The bottom right of the motif refers to the processes (activity systems). The distinction in the motif between core business processes, core support processes, and organizational support processes must be noted. The core business processes are those processes primarily tasked with the main purpose of the business. Examples are a bakery, which bakes, and being a telecommunication organization, it is to connect people. The core support processes refer to functional departments like marketing, sales, distribution, research, development, and others. In the final instance, organizational support processes refer to internal processes mainly concerned with preserving the organization as an entity. Human resource management, financial management, and information technology are typical examples of such processes. In Figure 7.1, the bottom left quadrant refers to the profit formula of the organization resulting from its strategic approach selected. The latter being either cost-leadership or differentiation (cf. Figure 2.2 combined with Step 3 of the strategy continuum).

Important to note at this stage that a value proposition cannot be changed as a stand-alone component of the business model. Rather, it is the outcome of what has changed in the activity processes component of the business model. Equally, the profit formula is an outcome of how effective and efficient resources are being applied, and, resources, as mentioned, are generic by nature.

It is therefore argued that the only component that can be changed with a significant impact on the rest of the model, is that of the activity processes.

The hypothesis of the authors is that a higher level of cultural competence will lead to higher organizational performance; the activity process part of the business model is where cultural competence needs to be added as the "drop of ink" in a glass of water.

Behavior is something we do, the human element of an organization. Therefore, it is argued that if we increase our CCI through an enhanced culturally competent behavioral approach, nestled in the activity processes component of the business model, depicted in Figure 7.1, the impact will be felt in the other components of the model, in an equally positive manner, specifically in the value proposition and profit model.

The authors now move to the implementation of cultural competence and institutionalization thereof as described thus far. For this, reference is made to Kotter's Eight Steps (Kotter, 2012), and the Kanter Change Wheel (Kanter, 2011).

Kotter's Eight Step Change Process

Few people managed to simplify the complex process of change management the way John Kotter did through the development of his renowned

Eight Step process. These Eight Steps have been chosen to use this process as a relatively easy, yet highly effective and detailed framework to structurally drive the mindset change required amongst the leadership and staff members of an organization, supporting a cultural competence increase and higher CCI performance rating.

> John Paul Kotter is the Konosuke Matsushita Professor of Leadership, Emeritus, at the Harvard Business School, an author, and the founder of Kotter International, a management consulting firm based in Seattle and Boston. He is a thought leader in business, leadership, and change and is best known for his creation of the Eight Step Change Management Process.

Figure 7.2 illustrates the steps in combined themes, as well as individually.

Kotter is of the view that in order for everybody to buy into the change initiative, the **first step** is that a sense of urgency needs to be created by the leadership of an organization and communicated with everyone. This can sometimes prove to be difficult as different people see different things and see things differently. To help in this regard, it is necessary to get the change the vision right, which is the **third step** of the first stage. Kotter also emphasizes that the change in vision is significantly different from the organizational vision, and needs to be treated separately, but contributory to the longer-term vision of the organization. As for the **second step** of the first stage, Kotter argues that change is not to be led as a solo flight. To be successful, the change

Eight-step process for leading successful change

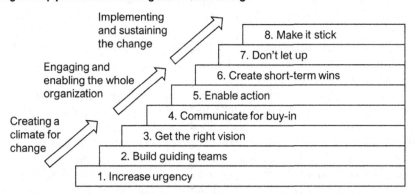

Figure 7.2 Kotter's Eight Step Process (Kotter, 2012). Illustration created by Marina van Zyl.

driver will need a team that he or she can rely on to assist in driving the change forward and overcome possible resistance to the change.

Note that there are three themes/stages to the process:

- Creating a climate for change
- Engaging and enabling the whole organization
- Implementing and sustaining the change

The first stage includes three steps:

- Increase urgency
- Build guiding teams
- Get the vision right

The company Microsoft is being used as an example to illustrate the above stages correlating with the CCI model.

Stage One

As an illustration of what is required to create a climate for change, the authors refer to Microsoft as a case study, discussed in Chapter Four (cf. pg. 47). Note that the sense of urgency created was not the urgency of increasing the CCI performance of the organization, but the need to 'take back' the leadership position the organization held in the industry prior to the Steve Balmer era. Failing this, the organization faced possible further losses and even extinction, judging by the market capitalization trend (cf. Figure 4.1) it followed at the time of Nadella's appointment as CEO. The method applied to achieve the success Microsoft achieved under Nadella's leadership, however, focuses on human elements. It is argued that a strong dose of cultural competence has been the focus. Comparing what Nadella did to the constructs of the variables of the CCI (cf. Figure 5.5), there is a close resemblance between his focus and the constructs.

The financial performance variable includes globally standardized indices as constructs, as per the CCI framework. Microsoft, being a listed company, followed these indices.

The internal stakeholders' loyalty variable includes staff, governance, and support, as constructs. Nadella focused on Microsoft's staff to break the previous culture of internal competition and target-focused behavior, where staff would 'step on one another' to get recognized for higher rewards in the organization. Nadella institutionalized diversity and inclusion, a key driver of cultural competence, by incorporating it into the governance structures of the organization. Nadella ensured that recruitment was aligned with appointing the right people in the right positions and in the right geographical areas of Microsoft's envisioned growth.

By applying his growth mindset, Nadella enabled the forming of a guiding team. People that bought into his new vision for the organization and contributed to establishing the right culture for change. Nadella's change vision was a different internal staff culture and a more informed client culture.

The second part of the vision formulation followed the same ingredient contribution of the external stakeholders' loyalty variable constructs. These are buyers, suppliers, and the government (cf. pg. 56).

Nadella insisted that his staff leave their office and spend more time with the customers (buyers), determining their real current and future needs. Supplier relationships were strengthened and relationships with governments were pursued in the lure of potential future cloud-hosting services.

In summary, the change vision for Microsoft was a different internal and external human relational organization. For this, cultural competence was a critical success ingredient. The organizational vision was reclaiming market lead through growth and customized solutions. A shift from a profit-centric to a customer-centric approach (cf. Figure 2.3) was idealized as an organizational vision.

Stage Two

The second stage of Kotter's change process is to engage and enable the organization as a whole. This consists of two separate steps:

- Enable action
- Communicate for buy-in

The Microsoft example can be clearly observed from the case study analysis presented in Chapter Four, indicating how Nadella communicated not just his vision, but the creation of a new kind of organization. For this he self-authored a book; 'Hit Refresh', 2017. In it, he associates with his staff through personalized stories of growth in empathy, a key ingredient for the effective adoption of personal cultural competence. He walks a further mile to enable action by adopting a growth mindset in listening to his female executives, further improving his empathy, and embracing diversity and inclusion. Both the latter are strong components of enhanced levels of personal cultural competence.

Stage Three

The third stage in Kotter's change process is implementing and sustaining the change. This stage consists of three steps:

- Create short-term wins

- Do not let up
- Make it stick

Nadella realized that part of the success of the change initiative in Microsoft would be to engage staff. Staff engagement, resulting in staff loyalty, is a key component in standard sustainability reporting. It also happens to be a critical variable construct element when measuring the CCI (cf. pg. 56–57). Creating short-term wins and rewarding people for their effort and contribution positively contributes toward the creation of engaged and loyal staff. At this point, corporate governance can also be used to assist in the structural implementation of cultural competence.

Kanter's Change Wheel

Before adding structure to the design logic changes (cf. Chapter Five), supporting the cultural change initiative, it was considered worthwhile to also consider some components of Kanter's Change Wheel.

Two perspectives are argued. The first perspective supports Kotter's change process and is a secondary source. The second perspective is depicted in Figure 7.3. The ten-spoke wheel contains some elements which bear a close relation to what was discovered by the authors through

Figure 7.3 Kanter's Change Wheel (Kanter, 2011). Illustration created by Marina van Zyl.

thorough research and positively contribute toward the improvement in organizational CCI performance.

Rosabeth Moss Kanter is the Ernest L. Arbuckle professor of business at Harvard Business School. She is also the director and chair of the Harvard University Advanced Leadership Initiative. She is the creator of the Kanter Change Wheel.

In analyzing the fourth spoke of education, training, and action tools as an example, this step/spoke can assist people to know what to do to make the change operational, to make it real in their activities. For diverse staff members, the selection of educational methods, training, and tools might in all likelihood be different. Because of diversity, the same words can sometimes be understood differently by staff from different cultural backgrounds and different parts of the organization. It might even be interpreted from their own perspectives, leading to differences.

To overcome these challenges, cultural competence needs to be considered in the design of the educational, training, and tools selection stage. This step is necessary to communicate the *why* and *what* of change for an understanding of the goal and its rationale and to enable and better equip them to envision and execute new actions. Training is also necessary for leading to adept at the new behavior implied by the change; in this case, a culturally competent change behavior. This step is critical to shape and guide behavior.

To understand the proposed design logic changes, reference is made to the process(es) component of the business model, depicted in Figure 7.1.

In most organizations, the organizational support processes are fairly generic, being Human Resources, Information Technology, and Finance. These activity systems are self-directed and concerned with maintaining the organization as an entity. The core activity systems are outward-directed and concerned with the main reason the business exists. The core support activity systems are inward-directed and assist the core processes to perform better. It thus makes sense to structurally add cultural competence in an institutionalized format to the organizational support activity systems; the reason being, as can be seen here in Figure 7.4, the organizational support processes flow into both the core and core support processes.

Ensuring that cultural competence spreads like a "drop of ink" through a glass of water, is most effective when positioning it as an organizational support process when implementing it through the corporate governance structure of the organization.

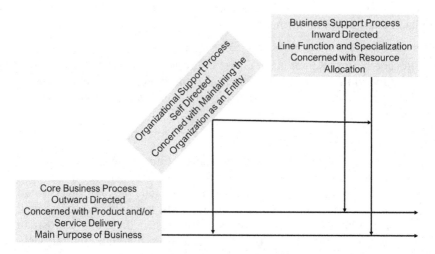

Figure 7.4 Organizational Activity Systems: Amended (Dostal, Cloete, & Jaros, 2005). Illustration created by Marina van Zyl.

This concludes the explanation on implementing cultural competence as both a cultural/behavioral change initiative in an organization, as well as a structural design logic change element.

Chapter Seven: Key Takeaways

- Cultural competence can be institutionalized by focusing on the process component of a business model.
- Profit formula, value proposition, and resources, as the other three components of a business model cannot be changed in isolation but result in changes if process components are changed.
- Kotter's Eight-Step Change Process can be used to guide organizations through a change management process, implementing both cultural and structural changes necessary to implement cultural competence into the organization.
- Because of diversity, the same words can sometimes be understood differently by staff from different cultural backgrounds and different parts of the organization.
- The components of a change management process are closely related to the constructs of the CCI performance measurement matrix.

Chapter 8

Future Challenges and Opportunities for Cultural Competence

Introduction

Having completed the narrative on cultural competence as an internal competitive differentiator, ensuring longer-term holistic sustainable competitiveness, a description of future challenges and opportunities for cultural competence is described in this chapter. Some future challenges on the horizon are explored with reference to the age of digitization, artificial intelligence, connectedness, distributed workforce, virtual management, virtual teams, and other exciting developments in the foreseeable future. These are related to the importance of embracing cultural competence as an internal strategic differentiator.

This chapter is presented as an opinion of the authors, deducting viewpoints and arguments based on the research conducted for the purposes of authoring the book. The aim is to motivate organizational leaders to put thought processes in place on the concept(s) of cultural competence to constantly consider ways of improving work-life practices between diverse human cultures, in a structured way.

The aim of this chapter is thus to not remain focused on the strategic competitiveness advantages of cultural competence only but to ensure that the reader has a wider perspective on cultural competence for life in general.

The age of digitization, connectedness, and cultural competence is referred to in the next discussion.

From the early 20th century initiation of the first industrial revolution to where we are today, one thing remains certain, technology has not just changed how we do things, it has changed human beings. Medical science improved and there is an increase in life expectancy through research and development into technology. COVID-19 vaccinations were developed in a record-breaking time and probes were dispatched into orbit around Mars. The question is, did humans not perhaps disconnect from each other?

The question arises as to what is meant by this latter part of the *entrée* into this chapter's points of discussion.

DOI: 10.4324/9781003303381-9

It is commonly mentioned that human beings live in the most connected-disconnected area at all times. It is true that technology has made connection across borders globally much more possible, but at the same time family dinner times have to compete with addicted face timers, as teenagers, and parents alike, find it impossible to let go of the so-called smart device. People drop attention to listening to a discussion at the first sound of the device's ringtone and are happy to be interrupted by a telephone call, expecting everyone to understand, depicting this behavior as 'normal.'

Tying these points of discussion together, it is explored what has digitization, connectedness, and cultural competence to do with one another. To unpack this statement/question posed, the reader is referred to the Airbnb case study discussed in Chapter Three (cf. pg. 31). The human characteristic that Airbnb managed to address, and create, although that being in a digital space, mostly, was that of trust. However, trust, it is said, requires physical proximity to be established. And trust is a key contributor, as well as an outcome, of cultural competence. Exercising cultural competence is with the aim of reaching a level of trust between diverse people where one can trust the other. In cultural competence, this is of specific importance and value as cultural competence is not about a list of behavioral dos and don'ts. It is about establishing a trust to the level that, when people are culturally incompetent toward one another, but not out of intent, but rather in the attempt of goodwill, they are forgiven, and shown/taught the culturally appropriate way.

Part of the challenge cultural competence faces is related to digitization, described by the authors as 'pseudo connectedness' and its limitation of establishing the kind of trust referred to. As a practical example, reference is made to the Digitization Transformational success of the Development Bank of Singapore Limited, commonly known as DBS (Sia, Weill, & Zhang, 2021). DBS Bank Ltd, based in Marina Bay, Singapore, is a Singaporean multinational banking and financial services corporation, whose Digital Transformation success has led to numerous case study teachings being done on the back of its success. It is important to think wider than only about strategic competitiveness. One of the successful initiatives was the way in which the bank changed its manner in connecting with its customers over time. This change being from a profit-centric inside-out approach to today's customer-centric outside- approach (cf. Figure 2.3). DBS managed to utilize its systems to allow digital channel connectivity and most banking services, provided previously at a physical branch, could now be done whilst customers had time to 'kill.'

This contributed to improving the bank's competitiveness, market share, and shareholder return.

It could however be a challenge that this method of connecting with customers, them having to deal increasingly with a digital application, is mutually inclusive of not connecting with an organization, let alone with a person. This form of digitization breaks with the traditional relationship-building practice of establishing trust between people. One representing the organization, the other being the customer. It is also argued that trust might be impacted on negatively and resulting in less customer loyalty. Not that it is a critical success factor necessary for customers to transact, but it is just a factor of absence in terms of measuring customer loyalty as part of the external stakeholder dimension of the CCI.

The authors are of the view that this kind of 'connected-disconnectedness' between organizations and their customers, has the potential to expose organizations to the risk of competitors starting to compete on better digital applications, and not necessarily on enhanced product and/or service delivery. The DBS case study illustrates how better digital services do not by default lead to a correlated positive increase in trust and loyalty. It only proves that it leads to a better customer experience. If a competitor competes with the experience by providing a better digital application experience, it is loyalty urging customers/people to stay, not the experience itself. And for trust and loyalty, cultural competence is required.

Considerations/questions for organizational leaders

- How sure are you that your digitization efforts lead to higher levels of trust and customer loyalty?
- Are you ensuring that cultural competence addresses issues between diverse customers to establish authentic human relationships, not just application-based transactional ones?
- Digitization is here to stay and has changed us, the human species. Do you know and are you sure whether your customers are trusting you; or trusting your technology?
- Consider after internalizing the concepts of this book to use your CCI and classification matrix measurements on the various CCI variables and constructs to continuously improve people's elements of trust and loyalty, even though connectedness is functional mainly through applications.
- Loyalty and trust require physical proximity – be 'on the floor with your customers'!

Artificial Intelligence and Cultural Competence

There are however viewpoints and opinions to raise around challenges and opportunities cultural competence faces when it has to cross the bridge to artificial intelligence. The opinions raised focus on both artificial intelligence as well as human intelligence, within the ambit of cultural competence.

Some definitive description(s) of intelligence are alluded to, to standardize the meaning of the terminology used.

Human intelligence is generally defined as the ability to solve complex problems or make decisions with outcomes benefiting the 'actor.' This form of intelligence has evolved in lifeforms to adapt to diverse environments for their survival and reproduction.

Artificial intelligence (AI) being the ability of a computer or a robot, controlled by a computer, to do tasks that are usually done by humans because they require human intelligence and discernment. In this sense, AI refers to the simulation of human intelligence in machines that are programmed to think like humans and mimic their actions. This is done by using algorithms and programming.

The authors' viewpoint of interest and line of thought is that AI is built to think like humans and mimic their actions. Can one actually comprehend how immense the implication is of teaching a computerized machine to mimic human actions and think like humans? One such implication the authors provide as food for thought is which human's thoughts and behaviors will be those to be mimicked and who will decide that? Which human thought paradigm and actions will be the blueprint to AI? Is each nation, culture, nationality, tribe, or diverse grouping of humans, going to have their own? And, if so, how is AI progressing? If we as a human species, planetary inhabitants, have not shown in our history and existence on earth that we can get along; that we can co-exist with other humans and with nature; that we can unite and not just divide; that we can open borders and not build walls; that we are truly there for one another in caring and sharing; then what part of our actions and thoughts are intelligent?

The authors argue that if cultural competence is the successful application of cultural interests, awareness, understanding, sensitivity, and intelligence (cf. Chapter One), it should be a key dimension added to the creation of AI. The reason for this argument being that the very essence of cultural competence is not the superiority of one culture over another, but one of learning from one another. Cultural competence defies the continuance of separatist and nationalist superiority by belief, and culture, and some people's unwillingness to learn from one another. It aims to connect complex worldviews of ingrained systemic cultural differences and ideologies, advocating the belief of superiority over others, and finds ways of co-existence.

Many are still wary when it comes to AI, claiming that futuristic movies of machine destruction to humankind are a real possibility in the advent of AI. However, the authors believe that the biggest threat of AI is still the intelligence part, not the artificial part. As it is the intelligence part that refers to mimicking human action and thinking like humans, not the artificial part. And to overcome this, it is recommended that a strong sense of cultural competence be the forerunner as humankind ventures into a future that holds the promise of AI integration into humankind's existence in everyday communities.

Distributed Workforce, Virtual Management, and Virtual Teams

Certainly, no one doubts the changes in our working lives after COVID-19. What has been accentuated however, is the increased need for cultural competence due to the increased level of internationalization, forced through the state of global lockdowns during the pandemic. During this time, international companies could not recruit expatriates due to travel bans and efforts had to be made to employ local talent in host countries to fill vacancies where needed. Whereas it was seen to be an intermediate action at the time, the prolonged state of lock-down institutionalized many of these practices and the multicultural composition of workforces globally persists today still. Some challenges in cultural competence, when referring to distributed workforces, virtual management, and virtual teams, relate to the necessity of trust and the required physical proximity necessary to build such trust. It is interesting to note that trust appeared to have been an issue even before virtual management and WFA practices became popular. Post the lock-down period, it became evident that, once the global restrictions were lifted, many managers and leaders wanted their workforce 'back where they could see' them. This, it turned out, was exactly because of the lack of trust, and not because of a critical factor for increased performance or need to provide direction and leadership in the presence of a physical space. Cultural competence in a virtual world has become an even higher critical factor for organizational success, as management by presence is becoming something of a dwarfing practice. If trusting one's own employees is a challenge for organizations, how much more will it not be for a virtual internationalized workforce and world-of-work all together? The current world of work faces challenges of how to on-board new employees virtually, for example. How to build high-performing teams 'in the cloud' is another example of an emergent challenge. How to have difficult conversations and coach people? How to have that all-important sit-down face-to-face conversation, so needed, and something had gotten used to? Clearly, cultural competence as an approach to working virtually is becoming more relevant and critical as we aim to address these challenges.

Chapter Eight: Key Takeaways

- Life is lived in the most digitized era of all times.

- Trust remains one of the biggest challenges to organizational success.
- Virtual connection only with customers leaves organizations vulnerable to competition of a technical nature, not just a product and/or service nature.
- Connectedness through applications is mistaken for loyalty.
- The textbook on how to establish trust within a distributed workforce, virtual management, and virtual teams still has many blank pages.

Epilogue

The key challenge that organizations face today in a fast-changing world and one where the fundamentals of business are being challenged with new technologies, changing world of work and labor markets, globalization, and customer/consumer behaviors – is simply to stay competitive. Competitiveness has been traditionally a function of differentiated products and services as well as, naturally, cost-effectiveness.

The economic system created since the mid-eighties has been one which has leveraged on globalization, open markets, and extended supply chains and which was supported by improved logistics and created greater cost value competitiveness. Furthermore, technology has helped reduce the cost of production through mainly mass production systems which in turn created greater supply, and reduced costs but inevitably also increased non-sustainable consumerism. This has all started to change with a greater focus on sustainable production, environmentally friendly, socially responsible, and generally Environmental, Social and Governance (ESG) performance monitoring and voluntary sustainability reporting by organizations around the world.

The challenges, however, still very much remain for organizations in that all these *external environment-related* dimensions can only be reacted to, or at best somewhat planned for. They can only be managed and in many ways when applying reactionary or even planned strategies, competition can also catch up and compete by imitating or providing similar products and service offerings.

What is difficult to imitate is creating a culture of organizational 'cultural competence' – which is something internal to an organization, very much part of its DNA and uniqueness, and a differentiator. The world has become bigger and more complex, especially in terms of, creating, sustaining, and growing a business. As such the authors have argued in this book that complexity is better served by diversity and not necessarily only by expertise. Whilst expertise and product/service knowledge are critical, it is something that can be developed easily or created through

DOI: 10.4324/9781003303381-10

attracting the right level of talent and bringing in the knowledge and skills into an organization, through talent acquisition and development.

Throughout this book, the authors endeavored to explain how cultural competence differs from cultural interest, awareness, understanding, sensitivity, and intelligence. Thus, cultural competence systematically impacts the entire organizational DNA and brings forth an emergent internal competitive advantage. With organizations focusing more in the past two decades on margin management and cost reduction to improve competitiveness, the authors have argued that this is short-termism at best and clearly not a sustainable look at the future development of an organization.

Externally, with organizational thinking being more focused on cost reduction and margin management at the detriment of the environment and other important socio-environmental considerations, we have created a very fragile global economy, and the supply chain issues during the 2020–2022 pandemic were clear testimony to that compromised global economic system.

Back to more internal factors thinking, it is clearly explained how cultural competence creates internal differentiation as opposed to external product and service differentiation. Ultimately organizations that develop their internal cultural competence strength, become truly differentiated and can develop an exceedingly difficult-to-imitate, internal strength.

This is clearly a strategic enabling component for an organization and one which transcends that traditional sustainable competitiveness model which is achieved by organizations through scale and scope management as prescribed by most of the business schools. Sustainable competitiveness is thus pursued by many organizations through the exploitation of scale and scope as very much directed in most of the schools of thinking in the business world.

The authors believe that many organizations do not realize how an internal strength can be leveraged in their positioning with respect to competitors. This is significant because if the focus is more on products and services alone; then the diversification of resources is mainly to exploit benefits from the international labor practices and their economic implications. Through understanding better, the human elements and systems of organizational stakeholders including suppliers, buyers, regulators, and other stakeholders; a differentiated way of outperforming competitors can be achieved.

The creation of more customer-centric relationships can create a more sustainable and meaningful relationship with customers whose commitment to a brand will be much more effective, and for this to happen cultural competence is essential. Furthermore, the authors have emphasized that cultural competence is a *way the organization is* rather a way that organization *is programmed through processes to be.*

Without an effective integration of cultural competence into the organization's strategy planning process(es) it is quite difficult to achieve the maximum effectiveness of an organization. Thus, the authors have explained that cultural competence needs to be structurally considered at every step/stage of strategy planning to achieve the outcomes desired. It is elaborated on how cultural competence impacts significantly on each of the five decisions which are made in a strategy continuum of what; where; how; implementation; and support.

Several valid case studies have been done to illustrate how companies have been more successful than others in different markets using more internal differentiators to achieve a more distinct and unique competitive advantage.

The framework for the moderation of culturally competent behaviors to result in influence that spans across the organization's transactional pipeline.

The strong correlation between an organization's ability to be more adaptive to cultural competence approaches with all its stakeholders and the maintenance of a growth mindset has been proven. In doing so these organizations continue to have a better and clearer understanding of what cultural competence is, how it remains as an internal competitive advantage, and also more importantly how the values of cultural competence and understanding are weaved to being part of the organization's true fabric. This is what makes it unique and difficult to imitate – which creates in turn an effective competitive advantage which in turn becomes an organizational strength.

It is interesting how organizations behaved very differently with their key internal stakeholders during the last pandemic. Some organizations continued to see the importance of investing in their people even in economically challenging times. Many of such organizations generally invest in their people, and focus on people-centric development beyond increased short-term performance – they retain talent and perform better and more sustainably as they see that eventually, and are thus more resilient. This then provides for a better more effective customer-centric organization, one which appreciates the cultural competence it has within and behaves thus with the customer with that same level of awareness and creates more meaningful connections with customers and their needs.

In the retail and hospitality industry, we have seen how the organizations that retained and tried to continue to train their workforce, exhibited much better service levels and customer services as organizations in different geographies started to emerge from the pandemic. Others which had to rehire and start to train and retrain lost on their customer experience offering which was clearly felt. It could be argued that the more culturally competent organizations had a better holistic understanding and approach and continued to maintain their values through as they say, through 'thick and thin' most trying times.

What is difficult to measure is difficult to manage as well. Methods are offered in this book to measure and quantify cultural competence to help with planning and improvement. The methods measure in quantitative terms and the scoring methodologies are very much based on qualitative assessments.

A significant aspect of the discussion has been that there is a weaker correlation than one may think between national culture and cultural competence. So, whilst there is the case for a national culture being embraced as a way of competing and a route to holistic sustainable competitiveness by any leader, generally this is linked more to the willingness to regard cultural diversity as a primary source of learning.

The Cultural Competence Index (CCI) embraces and links to other well-established thinking and models such as the work of Hofstede's entry modes and Porter's Five Forces and others. It must be appreciated that competence, in cultural competence, is measured through the CCI by determining the contribution that cultural competence makes in the success achieved, or not, in an organization's performance. Various case studies have been used to illustrate the application of the CCI and whilst the authors must emphasize that this is not an exact science, the incorporation of the human dimension and element into the traditional models such as Porter's Five Forces does assist leaders to enhance implementation of cultural competence aspects into the organizational workings.

In the closing chapters of this book, in-depth discussions are held around the enabling of continuous measurement of an organization's cultural competence contribution to holistic sustained completeness. The discussion focusses around understanding the critical success factors and initialization of cultural competence within an organization and thus the significance of change management, making reference to Kanter's Change Wheel and Kotter's Eight Steps process of change – effectively transforming over time an organization's DNA!

The authors conclude with looking at the challenges and opportunities for cultural competence in the context of ensuring long-term sustainable competitiveness. Leaders must genuinely believe that cultural competence is what will develop the internal competitive advantage and will make them a stronger and more resilient organization. The future challenges include digitization and digital transformations; artificial intelligence and how it will be leveraged; connectedness and communications; distributed workforce and virtual management of teams, and other significant transformational developments facing every leader. Soft and hard skills are meaningfully being brought to the fore in the different case studies, scenarios, and findings.

The authors, however, continue to argue for the importance of embracing cultural competence as an internal strategic differentiator.

Bibliography

Ackoff, R. L. (1989). From data to wisdom. *Journal of Applies Systems Analysis*, 3–9. Retrieved from https://www.systems-thinking.org/dikw/dikw.htm

Aguilar, F. (1967). *Scanning the Business Environment*. Macmillan, New York.

Alves, J. C., Lovelace, K. J., Manz, C. C., Matsypura, D., Toyasaki, F., & Ke, K. (2006). A cross-cultural perspective of self-leadership. *Journal of Managerial Psychology*, 22.

Ang, S., Van Dyne, L., Koh, C., Ng, Y. K., Templer, K. J., Tay, C., & Chandrasekar, A. N. (2007). Cultural intelligence: Its measurement and effects on cultural judgment and decision making, cultural adaptation and task performance. *Management and Organization Review*, 38.

Canen, A. G., & Canen, A. (2002). Innovation management education for multicultural organisations: challenges and a role for logistics. *European Journal of Innovation Management*, 13.

Cheng, L.-R. L. (2007). Communication disorders quarterly. *Communication Disorders Quarterly*, 8.

Collard, J. (2007). Constructing theory for leadership in intercultural contexts. *Journal of Educational Administration*, 16.

Dhupia, S., Kumar, P., & Sahijwani, R. (2020). When the world changed: A leader's Journal Through Covid-19. *Harvard Business Publishing Corporate Learning*.

Dong, L., & Glaister, K. W. (2009). Antecedents of perceived national and corporate culture differences: evidence from Chinese international strategic alliances. *Asia Pacific Business Review*, 26.

Dostal, E., Cloete, A., & Jaros, G. (2005). *Biomatrix: A Systems Approach to Organisational Societal Change 3rd Edition*. BiomatrixWeb.

Earley, C. P., & Ang, S. (2006). Cultural intelligence: Individual inter-actions across cultures. *Academy of Management Review*, 6.

Esty, B., & Fisher, D. (2019). The a2 Milk Company. *Harvard Business School*.

Fray, A. M. (2007). Ethical behavior and social responsibility in organizations: process and evaluation. *Management Decision*, 13.

Goleman, D. (1995). *Emotional Intelligence*. Bantam Books.

Graf, A., & Mertesacker, M. (2009). Intercultural training: Six measures assessing training needs. *Journal of European Industrial Training*, 20.

Harris, H., & Kumra, S. (2000). International manager development: Cross-cultural training in highly diverse environments. *Journal of Management Development,* 13.

Helms, M., & Nixon, J. (2010). Exploring SWOT Analysis - where are we now? *Journal of Strategy and Management,* 215–251.

Hofstede, G. (1993). Cultural constraints in management theories. *Academy of Management Executive,* 16.

Jansson, H., Johanson, M., & Ramström, J. (2007). Institutions and business networks: A comparative analysis of the Chinese, Russian, and West European markets. *Industrial Marketing Management,* 13.

Jassawalla, A., Truglia, C., & Garvey, J. (2004). Cross-cultural conflict and expatriate manager adjustment. *Management Decision,* 13.

Johnson, J. P., Lenartowicz, T., & Apud, S. (2006). Cross-cultural competence in international business. *Journal of International Business Studies,* 20.

Johnson, J. P., Lenartowicz, T., & Apud, S. (2006). Cross-cultural competence in international business: Toward a definition and a model. *Journal of International Business Studies,* 19.

Johnson, M., Christensen, C., & Kagermann, H. (2008). Reinventing your business model. *Harvard Business Review,* 86.

Jose, A. C. (2006). A cross-cultural perspective of self leadership. *fojwoivjd,* 22.

Kanter, R. (2011). The change wheel: Elements of systemic change and how to get change rolling. *Harvard Business School.*

Kim, K., Kirkman, B. L., & Chen, G. (2006). Cultural intelligence and international assignment effectiveness. *Academy of Management Best Conference Paper,* 9.

Kotter, J. (2012). *Leading Change.* Harvard Business Review Press.

Kuhlmann, T., & Hutchings, K. (2010). Expatriate assignments vs localization of management in China. *Career Development International,* 19.

Lafley, A., & Martin, R. (2013). How Strategy Really Works. In A. Lafley, & R. Martin, *How Strategy Really Works.* Harvard Business Review Press.

Lee, L.-Y., & Croker, R. (2006). A contingency model to promote the effectiveness of expatriate training. *Industrial Management & Data Systems,* 19.

Lessem, R. (2001). Managing in four worlds: Culture, strategy and transformation. *Long Range Planning,* 24.

Luthans, K. W., & Farner, S. (2002). Expatriate development: The use of 360-degree feedback. *Journal of Management Development,* 14.

Mayo, A., & Nohria, N. (2005). *In Their Time: The Greatest Business Leaders of the Twentieth Century.* Harvard Business Review Press.

Muzychenko, O. (2008). Cross-cultural entrepreneurial competence in identifying international business opportunities. *European Management Journal,* 12.

Narayandas, D., Margolis, J., & Raffaelli, R. (2017). Ron Johnson: A Career in Retail. *Harvard Business School.*

Porter, M. (2008). The five competitive forces that shape strategy. *Harvard Business Review.*

Shapiro, J. M., Ozanne, J. L., & Saatcioglu, B. (2008). An interpretive examination of the development of cultural sensitivity in international business. *Journal of International Business Studies,* 17.

Shi, X., & Wright, P. C. (2000). Developing and validating an international business negotiator's profile. *Journal of Managerial Psychology, 26.*

Sia, S., Weill, P., & Zhang, N. (2021). Designing a future ready enterprise: The digital transformation of DBS Bank. *California Management Review, 63.*

Sizoo, S., Plank, R., Iskat, W., & Serrie, H. (2005). The effect of intercultural sensitivity on employee performance in cross-cultural service encounters. *Journal of Services Marketing, 11.*

Tahiri, J. (2017). Slx Sigma: A Case Study in Motorola. www.pecb.com.

Tams, S., & Arthur, M. B. (2007). Studying careers across cultures - Distinguishing international, cross-cultural, and globalization perspectives. *Career Development International, 13.*

Tan, J.-S. (2004). Cultural intelligence and the global economy. *LIA, 4.*

Thomas, D. A. (2004). Diversity as strategy. *Harvard Business Review, 12.*

van Veenhuyzen, C. (2008). Self, other and social contexts. *Eskom Resources and Strategy Division, 18.*

Welch, J. (2016, June 1). My Greatest Leadership Learnings From a Life in Business. (P. Sumit, Interviewer).

Index

Note: Page numbers in **Bold** refer to tables; and page numbers in *italics* refer to figures

Ackoff, R. L. 1, *1*, 15, 17
Ackoff's model. *see* Data, Information, Knowledge, and Wisdom (DIKW) Model
Aguilar, F. J. 4, 5, 33
Airbnb, Inc. 34–36, 90
Amazon Prime 3, 28
a2 Milk Company Limited 72–75
Apple Inc. 16
artificial intelligence (AI) 9, 49, 89, 91–93, 98

Baker, G. F. 16
Ballmer, S. 48, 49
BASF SE company 46
Biomatrix Systems Theory 42
Biomatrix Web 42
Blockbuster LLC 37
Boston Consulting Group (BCG) 75–76
Burberry 71
Burger King 3, 28
business model 81, *81*
business-model centric innovation 27

Caffe Nero 3
castling 18, 24, 32–47
CCI measurement matrix: application of 68–69; buyers 71–72; classification matrix (CM) 64–68; conceptual and structural positioning 60, *60*; external stakeholder 61, 62, *62*, 70; financial reporting explanation 78; governance explanation 77–78;

government/other stakeholders 72–75; internal stakeholder 62, *63*, 70; overview 57–59; positioning cultural competence 59–64; scorecard categories 59; simpler version 69, *69*; staff 75–76, *77*; support explanation 78; sustainability reporting 79
Christensen, C. M. 81
Christensen, C. R. 16
classification matrix (CM) 59, 64, 65, 70, 91; constructs and elements 65–66; overview 64; in practices 66–68; staff performance cultural competence dimension **77**; supplier/landlord 65, *66*; supplier performance cultural competence dimension **67**
Coca-Cola 3, 28
competitiveness 95, 96
conventional differentiator approach 39
Costa 3
Country Road Group 40
COVID-19 12, 20, 26, 75, 89, 93
cultural awareness 13, 17, 72
cultural competence: Ackoff's model 15, 17; competitive advantage 11; Cultural Competence Index (CCI) 8; culture and civilization 11; definition 2, 18; difficult-to-penetrate strategy 18; distributed workforce 93; dual transformation 51–52; future challenges and opportunities 89–94;

institutionalization of 9; internal
competitive advantage 2, 6;
internal strategic differentiator 9;
KPA performance 65, 68; level of
wisdom 16–19; measurement tool
54–56, *55*; organizational culture
7; Porter's five forces model 3–4,
7, 22–24; realm 23, *23*; scalability
approach 11–12; situational
arrogance 16; stakeholder
components 3, 23; strategic value
7; strategy planning process 7;
sustained holistic competitiveness
8, 9, 21; systemic impact of 10;
trust and loyalty 91; virtual
management and virtual teams 93
Cultural Competence Index (CCI) 8, 45,
48, *55*, 57, 58, 98
cultural intelligence 2, 14–15, 17, 72
cultural interest 6, 10, 13, 15, 52, 72,
92, 96
cultural understanding 13–14, 65, 66,
68, 72
"culture eats strategy for breakfast"
28–29
customer-centric approaches *26*,
26–28, 56, 85
customer-centric relationships 96

Data, Information, Knowledge, and
Wisdom (DIKW) Model 1, *1*,
15, 16
David Jones 40
DBS Bank Ltd 90, 91
Dell Computer Company 44–45
Digital Transformation success 90
digitization, connectedness, and
cultural competence 89, 90
Disney 3, 28
Dostal, E. 42, 43
Drucker, P. F. 28
Dweck, C. S. 52

Edison, T. 10, 11
Enjoy Technology 16
Environment, Social & Governance
(ESG) 61, 95

FedEx 3, 28
Fonterra Co-operative Group
Limited 73

Galvin, B. 29
Galvin, P. 29
Galvin, R. W. 29
Goldman Sachs 48, 49
governance 8, 44, 45, 47, 54, 59, 61,
62, 70, 71, 75–78, 84, 86,
87, 95
guarantees 21

Handy, C. 48
Harvard Business School (HBS) 16
Hastings, R. 36
The Hilton 35
Hit Refresh: The Quest to Rediscover
(Nadella) 49, 53, 85
Hofstede, G. 14, 15, 17, 54, 56
human intelligence 92
Humphrey, A. S. 4

Ibarra, H. 48
institutionalizing cultural competence:
activity system redesign 81–82;
business model 81, *81*;
communicate for buy-in 85;
enable action 85; external
stakeholders' loyalty 85;
implementing and sustaining the
change 85–86; internal
stakeholders' loyalty 84; Kanter's
Change Wheel *86*, 86–88; Kotter's
eight step process 82–84, *83*;
Nadella's leadership 84–85;
organizational activity systems 87,
88; overview 80

Johnson, R. 15, 16

Kanter, R. M. 9, 82, *86*, 86–88, 98
Kanter's Change Wheel *86*, 86–88
Kaplan, R. 54
Key Performance Areas (KPAs) 63–65,
68–70
Key Performance Indicators (KPIs) 44,
57, 59
Kotter, J. P. 9, 82–86, *83*, 98
Kotter's eight step process 82–84, *83*

Lafley, A.G. 32, 33

The Majid Al Futtaim Group 42
Martin, R. 32, 33

Mayo, A. J. 16
Mayo, T. 16
McDonalds 3, 28
Microsoft 48, 49, *50*, 51–53, 58, 84–86
Mindset: The New Psychology of Success (Dweck) 52
Motorola, Inc. 29
MTN Group Limited 37–38, 45
Murphy, T. S. 16

Nadella, S. N. 6, 48–53, 55, 84–86
National Islamic Front (NIF) 20
Netflix, Inc. 3, 28, 36–37
Nimeiry, J. 20
Nohria, N. 16
Norton, D. 54

organization's strategy planning process 7, 97

Pep Africa 42
Pepsi 3, 28
PEST analysis (political, economic, social, and technological) 4, 5, 33
PESTLE framework 5, 33
Porter, M. 3–5, 8, 15, 21–24, 27, 33, 43, 46, 52, 54, 56, 61, 62, 64, 70, 98
Porter's five forces framework 3–4, 7, 22–24, 43
Procter & Gamble 32
profit-centric approaches *25*, 25–26

Randolph, M. 36
Rattan, A 48
Reuters, T. 64
Rotman School of Management 32

'Satya Nadella at Microsoft: Instilling a growth mindset' (Ibarra, Rattan, and Johnston) 48
Satya Nadella case: breakthrough insight 55; culture programs and training 50–52; evolution of Microsoft's stock price 49, *50*; focus on customer centricity 53;

growth mindset 48–50; from 'know-it-all' to 'learn-it-all' 52–56
Schwab, C. 18
Schwab, K. M. 19
Shewhart, W. A. 30
Shoprite Holdings Ltd 42
Six Sigma culture 29–30
soft skills 8, 21, 22, 30, 46, 61
Starbucks 3
strategy and the strive for uniqueness 24–25
strategy continuum framework 32–34, *33*; contextual components 33, 34; physical positioning 36–38; resource requirements 45–46; strategic intent and aspiration 34–36; structures, processes, and activities 42–45, *43*; tailoring uniqueness (USP) 38–42, *39*, *40*; transactional components 33, 34
Sudan People's Liberation Army (SPLA) 20
SWOT analysis (strengths, weaknesses, opportunities and threats) 4, 5

Target Corporation 16
Thompson, J. W. 48
Tommy Hilfiger 71
transactional leadership 51

Ubuntu-centric approach 39
unique selling proposition (USP) 35, 38–39, 44, 46, 81
United Parcel Service (UPS) 3, 28

values, and strategic direction 42, *43*
van Zyl, M. 23, *25*, 26, *33*, *39*, *40*, *43*, 60, 62, 63, 66, 69, 81, 88

Walmart Inc. 26
Welch, J. F., Jr. 45
Woolworths Holdings Limited 40–42, 45, 64, 65, 68, 71
World Economic Forum (WEF) 19